MG MIDGET 1961-1980

Compiled by
R.M. Clarke

ISBN 0 946489 86 6

Distributed by
Brooklands Book Distribution Ltd.
'Holmerise', Seven Hills Road,
Cobham, Surrey, England

CONTENTS

ACKNOWLEDGEMENTS

When we produced our first book on the 'modern' Midget in 1979, I wrote that it hardly seemed possible that it had been with us for 18 years. Increduously it is now over five years since it went out of production and left a gap in the market which to date has not been filled.

There is however a bright side. Sprites and Midgets are being bought and cherished by young owners. They are being overhauled and rebuilt, raced and rallied and each year at shows in Britain, the United States and Australia their numbers are seen to increase.

Our series is targeted at these owners. They thirst for information about their cars and although the 'Classic' magazines cater for them, they also need the road tests and original model announcements relating to their vehicles.

Over the past 20 years, we have made available over 6,000 such articles for these enthusiasts. The motoring press has generously allowed us to reprint their copyright stories and our thanks in this instance go to the publishers of Autocar, Autosport, Car, Car and Driver, Cars & Car Conversions, Cars Illustrated, Collector's Car, Modern Motor, Motor, Road & Track, Sports Car Graphic, Sports Car World, World Car Catalogue and Wheels for their continued support.

We are also indebted to the owner of the Midget featured on our cover. We photographed it outside a delicatessen in Newport, Rhode Island, exactly a week after the Americas Cup sailed for Perth.

R.M. Clarke

THE MOTOR   July 12 1961

Motoring the Midget

The New Heir to an Old Title is Fun but far from Foolish

"NOW that you've tested the Mark II Sprite, why not have a go in a Midget?" That sort of invitation, issued in fine summer weather when you have just said a reluctant farewell to the Midget's twin brother, just doesn't get refused, so we enjoyed another 500 miles of motoring in another of the British Motor Corporation's sporting "babies."

If you want to read a Road Test Report on the new M.G. Midget, you will almost find one on pages 884-887 of this issue of *The Motor*. Almost, but by no means completely, because the Sprite and the Midget are not identical in specification, and because two nominally identical cars can be very different in character.

Apart from its M.G. emblems, the Midget has more thickly padded seats than the Sprite, which pleased some folk whereas those members of our staff who are large or have grown their own padding found that being pushed upwards and forwards slightly in the small cockpit was not an advantage. It has front floor covering of mottled plastic instead of ribbed rubber, and felt bonded to the underside of this plastic seems to do a useful noise-reducing job at speeds below 45 m.p.h. Another M.G. refinement concerns the rigid sidescreens, in which both front and rear halves of the window can slide open, instead of only the rear halves.

There is no design difference to account for it, but whereas our Sprite had a notice on the windscreen saying "100 Octane Petrol only" our Midget had an ignition setting with which it ran happily on ordinary Premium petrols. At speed, wind buffeting made both cars noisy, but around town the Midget was notably sweeter running—a steering gear with much less friction in it, and a freer gearchange, brought back all the old Sprite charm as a nimble town runabout, although above 60 m.p.h. the less sticky (but still completely positive) steering rack-and-pinion let the driver know about imperfections of front wheel balance.

We did not make full performance tests on the Midget, but its less sharply tuned engine seemed just as lively as the Sprite's in normal driving, even if a greater proportion of traffic motoring combined with its less-advanced ignition to increase its fuel thirst to about 31½ m.p.g. for our 540-mile test. Maximum speed seemed to be about 3 m.p.h. lower on this Midget than on the Sprite which we had been loaned, and to blame 1 m.p.h. apiece on less advanced ignition, on a canvas hood which is not so well streamlined as a hardtop, and on half as much running-in mileage (2,000 instead of over 4,000) would seem reasonable.

Under either identity, a Sprite or a Midget can be a most attractive possession. As a "trainer" for a young driver or fresh air tonic for an older one, as an entertaining "second car" to a saloon or as a temperament-free everyday transport, it offers a lot for a modest sum of money.

Interior differences to the Sprite include mottled plastic floor covering, thicker padded seats and rigid side screens on which both front and rear halves slide open.

M   1929-32   J2   1932-34   PB

1961 CARS

MIDGET
returns to
M.G. range

The First Under-1,000 c.c.
M.G. Since 1936

M.G. enthusiasts the world over will welcome the news that, for the first time since mid-1936—when the PB-type Midget went out of production—an under-1,000 c.c. model once again figures in the M.G. range.

The rationalization policy of the British Motor Corporation has been applied to its production and the new Midget is, in fact, one of a pair of basically similar models, the other being the recently introduced Mark II version of the Austin-Healey Sprite. In all their essentials the two cars are identical, but the Midget has a distinctive front, different trim and various de luxe items of finish and equipment not supplied on the standard version of the Mk. II Sprite.

Naturally it costs a little more, the basic price being £472 which, with British purchase tax of £197 15s. 10d., gives a home market total of £669 15s. 10d. This compares with the basic price of £445 (£631 10s. 10d. complete) asked for the Austin-Healey Sprite.

*   *   *

Power is supplied by a modified 2-carburetter version of the B.M.C. A-type engine, which has now been pro-duced to the tune of some 1,500,000 units. With a 9/1 compression ratio, it needs 100 octane fuel. The close-ratio four-speed synchromesh gearbox has a central remote-control lever.

Although a conventional rigid axle casing is used, the rear suspension is unusual in employing quarter-elliptic springs in conjunction with parallel, super-imposed radius arms—a system which has the advantages of low unsprung weight and of concentrating the main suspension loading on the centre portion of the unitary-construction shell, the tail playing no part in supporting the weight of the car. The sole functions of the latter are to carry the six-gallon rear tank and provide a useful luggage boot in which the spare wheel is housed horizontally on the floor.

At the front, conventional independent coil-and-wishbone suspension is used, embodying pressed-steel lower wishbones and single forged upper links that also serve as the arms of the lever-type Arm-strong hydraulic dampers. The steering gear is of the rack-and-pinion type.

The Midget has Lockheed hydraulic drum brakes with two leading shoes at the front; the handbrake is on the pas-senger's side of the propeller-shaft tunnel and has a normal (not "fly-off") ratchet button.

The new Midget is, of course, intended primarily as a two-seater, but there is a considerable space behind the two bucket seats; if required, a cushion can be sup-plied as an extra to enable this space to be used for carrying a youngster. Otherwise, it can be used for stowing coats, shopping and so on, and it will, in fact, take a good-sized suitcase.

The boot has a lockable lid and straps are provided on the bulkhead to secure the detachable hood material in an envelope clear of the floor. The separate hood sticks (which are of the two-piece type with a joint in the centre for easy stowage)

The
up,
on
wh

The spare wheel is stowed on the boot floor, but there is quite a fair amount of luggage space by sports-car standards.

Both bucket seats have sliding adjustment and the carpeted well behind them can take extra luggage. Flecked rubber matting covers the front floor. A large rev counter is standard; clutch and brake pedals are of pendant type, the throttle has an organ pedal.

TA/TB/TC 1936-49 TD 1950-53 TF 1953-55

also have their own envelope and fit round the spare wheel, still leaving a fair amount of room for luggage. With the additional space behind the seats in the passenger compartment, the Midget is very well provided with baggage space by sports car standards.

Unlike so many completely detachable hoods of the past, the new Midget design is neither difficult to erect nor deficient in vision—the latter thanks to a large rear window and sensibly-sized quarter lights, all in transparent plastic of the type which does not suffer from careless stowage. In addition, rigid-framed, sliding-panel side-screens can be fitted to the doors by quick-acting screws which can be operated with a coin. Both the forward and rear Perspex panels are arranged to slide.

The facia board is leathercloth covered, with a padded roll for the scuttle; a revolution counter is standard and both this and the speedometer (with total and trip mileage recorders) have a detailed scale. Other instruments comprise a fuel gauge, a water thermometer and an oil-pressure gauge. Toggle switches are used for the wipers and sealed-beam lights. Other accessories included as standard are a windscreen washer, anchorage points for safety belts and flasher-type direction indicators.

Among a long list of optional extras available from the factory are a radio set, a tonneau cover which can be arranged to cover the entire cockpit, to protect all but the driver's seat, or to cover the interior luggage space only, a heater and demister, and whitewall or heavy duty tyres; dealer-fitted accessories include a locking petrol cap, a cigar lighter, wing mirrors, twin horns, Ace Mercury wheel discs and a luggage carrier.

Externally, the new model is undeniably a good looker. Points special to the Midget include a very attractive front grille with vertical slats and the traditional M.G. trade mark incorporated in the central vertical bar, and embellishments in the form of a bright metal beading down the centre of the rear-hinged bonnet-top and a full-length flash on the body side; extending from the headlamps to the rear-light clusters, these flashes emphasize the low build. A total of five exterior colours, three types of interior trim and three hood colours are available in combinations which give a total of seven variants.

es quite good headroom, and is easy to put aturally looks at its sleekest when open, as picture below shows the special wheel trims ought as an extra and, carrying the M.G. ive the car a real *de luxe* appearance.

M.G. MIDGET SPECIFICATION

ENGINE	
Cylinders ...	4 in line with 3-bearing crankshaft.
Bore and stroke	62.9 mm. × 76.2 mm. (2.478 in. × 3.0 in.).
Cubic capacity ...	948 c.c. (57.87 cu. in.).
Piston area ...	19.29 sq. in.
Compression ratio	9/1.
Valvegear ...	In line o.h.v. operated by push rods and rockers.
Carburation ...	Two semi-downdraught S.U. type HS2 carburetters, fed by AC mechanical pump, from 6-gallon tank.
Ignition	12-volt coil, centrifugal and vacuum timing control, 14 mm. Champion N5 sparking plugs.
Lubrication ...	Tecalemit or Purolator external full-flow filter. Oil capacity 7 pints (incl. filter).
Cooling	Water cooling with pump, fan and thermostat; 10-pint water capacity (plus $\frac{1}{2}$ pint for heater if fitted).
Electrical system	12-volt, 43 amp. hr. battery charged by 19-amp. generator.
Maximum power	46.5 b.h.p. net (50 b.h.p. gross) at 5,500 r.p.m., equivalent to 2,750 ft./min. piston speed and 2.4 b.h.p. per sq. in. of piston area.
Maximum torque	52.5 lb. ft. at 2,750 r.p.m., equivalent to 138 lb./sq. in. b.m.e.p. at 1,375 ft./min. piston speed.
TRANSMISSION	
Clutch	Borg and Beck $6\frac{1}{4}$-in. single dry plate.
Gearbox ...	Four speeds with direct drive in top; synchromesh on three upper ratios.
Overall ratios ...	4.22, 5.726, 8.975 and 13.504; rev. 17.361.
Propeller shaft ...	Hardy Spicer, open.
Final drive ...	Hypoid bevel, three-quarter floating axle.
CHASSIS	
Brakes	Lockheed hydraulic, drum type all round.
Brake dimensions	Front and rear drums 7 in. dia. × $1\frac{1}{4}$ in. wide.
Brake areas ..	67.5 sq. In. of lining (33.75 sq. in. front and rear) working on 110 sq. in. rubbed area of drums.
Front suspension	Independent by coil springs and wishbones with Armstrong lever-arm dampers.
Rear suspension...	Quarter-elliptic leaf springs with parallel radius arms and Armstrong lever-type dampers.
Wheels and tyres	Ventilated disc wheels with 4-stud fixing and 5.20-13 tubeless tyres.
Steering	Rack and pinion.
DIMENSIONS	
Length	Overall 11 ft. $5\frac{5}{8}$ in.; wheelbase 6 ft. 8 in.
Width	Overall 4 ft. 5 in.; track 3 ft. $9\frac{3}{4}$ in. at front and 3 ft. $8\frac{3}{4}$ in. at rear.
Height	4 ft. $1\frac{3}{4}$ in.; ground clearance 5 in.
Turning circle ...	32 ft.
Kerb weight ...	14 cwt. (without fuel but with oil, water, tools, spare wheel, etc.).
EFFECTIVE GEARING	
Top gear ratio ...	15.4 m.p.h. at 1,000 r.p.m. and 30.6 m.p.h. at 1,000 ft./min. piston speed.
Maximum torque	2,750 r.p.m. corresponds to approx. 42.2 m.p.h. in top gear.
Maximum power	5,500 r.p.m. corresponds to approx. 84.0 m.p.h. in top gear.
Probable top gear pulling power...	190 lb./ton approx. (computed by *The Motor* from manufacturers' figures for torque, gear ratio and kerb weight, with allowances for $3\frac{1}{2}$ cwt. load, 10% losses and 60 lb./ton drag).

SPRITELY MIDGET

MG Midget and its twin, Sprite Mk. 2, offer sporty motoring for small outlay, says Doug Armstrong

B.M.C. spanned almost half a lifetime when they produced a new MG Midget last year.

The car that first made this name famous appeared in 1929 and was a development of the three-speed, overhead-camshaft Morris Minor; its 847c.c. engine pushed out 20 b.h.p., giving a top speed of about 60 m.p.h., and it cost £175 stg.

The latest Midget has a 948c.c., 46 b.h.p. engine, will top 85 m.p.h. in stock-standard form, and its basic price is £472 stg. Since the pound sterling today is worth at most a quarter of its 1929 value, this means you get a good deal more now, for

considerably less money, than you did in those days.

That's one of the benefits of modern mass-production methods and standardisation; but, on the debit side, buyers must be prepared to sacrifice much of the car's individuality.

The 1929 Midget was unique; nothing else could be mistaken for it on the road. The 1962 car has a twin brother — the Austin-Healey Sprite Mark II, which differs only in the styling of grille, wheels and badges.

In fact, both models are derived from the Mark I Sprite — completely

restyled at both ends and improved by replacing the forward-tipping bonnet-and-wings structure with a conventional fixed arrangement incorporating a normal alligator-type bonnet.

That tip-up front gave wonderful all-round accessibility to engine and suspension — but it was also prone to "shimmy," and there is no doubt that the new one-piece body. is far more rigid and less liable to develop squeaks and rattles. Also, the Sprite's original "bull-frog" look, with popped-up headlights and grinning grille, wasn't everyone's cup of tea, and the repositioning of headlights in the guards gets rid of that controversial feature.

Construction is unitary, of course—which, in the case of the Midget, makes it the first MG sports ever built without a separate chassis.

While redesigning the rear of the pressed-steel body shell, additional stiffening was provided at that end, too, by linking the side panels and wheel arches transversely with an 8in.-wide fixed "deck" blended into the uprights.

This enabled the designers to introduce an external-opening luggage boot (which the original Sprite lacked), still leaving a sizeable opening behind the twin bucket seats, where more luggage or a couple of young children can be carried.

Thus, despite the spare wheel, tools and folded soft hood which occupy much of the boot room, a lot of gear can be transported in the car —but I wouldn't bother getting the cushion for the occasional bench seat (an optional extra), because it reduces the space available in the rear

TWIN 1¼in. SU carbs extract 46 b.h.p. (net) at 5500 r.p.m. from 948c.c. A Series B.M.C. engine. Air-cleaners, screen-washer reservoir, heater-demister and battery (in scuttle) fill the little bay to capacity.

MIDGET looks equally neat as roadster (see sketch) or with the optional removable hardtop. Sprite differs only in grille. BELOW: Spare, tools, soft hood leave little room in boot; most luggage goes behind the seats.

Our Test Car

The MG Midget which B.M.C. lent me for testing was fitted with the optional hardtop—handsome and very easily attached by means of four neat clips. Like most removable hardtops, however, it emitted various clicks and creaks when under way.

The large rear window gave good visibility, and the alloy-framed side-screens (with sliding windows) also contributed to an above-average road view for this type of car.

It's a pity the side windows and hardtop weren't mated together better, as there were draught-admitting gaps alongside the windscreen pillars and between the hardtop and the top rear sections of the doors. I was thankful for the Smiths heater/demister, which kept the car's interior warm in England's bitterly cold January weather — even without switching on its booster motor.

Demisting of the windscreen was

compartment without serving any really useful purpose.

Mechanically, the new models differ from the Mark I Sprite in having larger carburettors, "hotter" camshafts, bigger valves, and a compression of 9 to 1 instead of 8.3 to 1 —though the old ratio is available as an option, for those who wish to (or must, as in Australia) use lower-grade fuel than 100-octane.

Gear ratios have also been respaced, improving the performance characteristics—but the synchro can still be beaten when changing down from top to third and third to second, while the non-synchromeshed first gear is harsh to engage, even at rest.

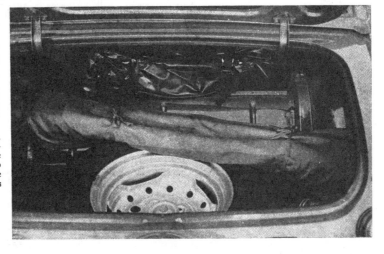

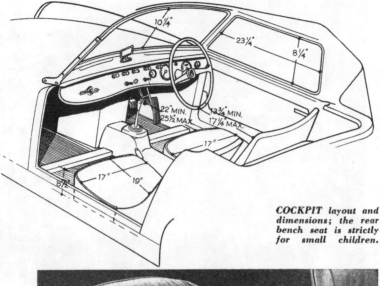

COCKPIT layout and dimensions; the rear bench seat is strictly for small children.

soon forgot or forgave them once we got out on the open road.

Performance, to use the road testers' favorite cliche, was exhilarating: from standstill, the Midget reached 60 in 19 seconds flat and hit 70 ten seconds later. Third gear, incidentally, can take it right up to 73 m.p.h.

Handling was good, the high-geared steering (2 1-3rd turns lock-to-lock) contributing greatly to ease of control and enjoyment of driving. The rack-and-pinion mechanism was a delight to handle; despite the high ratio, it was light at all speeds — a lesson to manufacturers of many other small cars with far lower-geared steering.

There were no flat-spots, and the engine was most responsive at all speeds; but I would have appreciated a bit more space between pedals, as I found that my "throttle foot" (a large one, admittedly) was apt to get trapped behind the brake pedal when the throttle was pressed well down.

The clutch was sweet throughout the test, and well up to racing-type take-offs and gear-changes.

No anti-roll bars are fitted to the MG Midget, and there is appreciable

(Continued on page 27)

SPECIFICATIONS

ENGINE: 4-cylinder, o.h.v.; bore 62.9mm., stroke 76.2mm., capacity 948c.c.; compression ratio 9.0 to 1; maximum b.h.p. 46 at 5500 r.p.m.; twin S.U. carburettors, mech. fuel pump; 12v. ignition.
TRANSMISSION: Single dry-plate clutch; 4-speed gearbox with synchromesh on top three; overall ratios—1st, 13.50; 2nd, 8.08; 3rd, 5.72; top, 4.22 to 1; reverse, 17.36 to 1; hypoid bevel final drive; 4.22 to 1 ratio.
SUSPENSION: Front independent, by unequal-length wishbones and coil springs; semi-elliptics at rear; lever-tyne shockers all round.
STEERING: Rack-and-pinion; 2 1-3rd turns lock-to-lock, 32ft. turning circle.
WHEELS: Pressed-steel discs, with 5.20 by 13in. tyres.
BRAKES: Lockheed hydraulic, 2 l.s. front; 110 sq. in. lining area.
CONSTRUCTION: Unitary.
DIMENSIONS: Wheelbase, 6ft. 8in.; track, front 3ft. 9¾in., rear 3ft. 8¾in.; length 11ft. 5⅝in., width 4ft. 6in., height 4ft. 0¾in.; ground clearance, 5in.
KERB WEIGHT: 13cwt.
FUEL TANK: 6 gallons.

PERFORMANCE

CONDITIONS: Extremely cold, no wind; smooth bitumen; two occupants, 100-octane fuel.
BEST SPEED: 86 m.p.h.
MAXIMUM in indirect gears: 2nd, 55 m.p.h.; 3rd, 73.
ACCELERATION from rest through gears: 0-30, 5.5s.; 0-40, 9.0s.; 0-50, 13.0s.; 0-60, 19.0s.; 0-70, 29.0s.
BRAKING: 31ft. 9in. to stop from 30 m.p.h. in neutral.
FUEL CONSUMPTION: 34 m.p.g.

very good, too, despite the unkind weather, but the rear window kept misting up and I had to reach back several times to wipe it with a cloth.

Driving position is quite good, though I would have appreciated thicker thigh padding on the bucket seats. The seat adjustment provides just enough leg-room for a six-footer, and there is no doubt that an "un-dished" steering wheel (and short-ened scuttle section) would make a tall driver more comfortable.

The instrument panel is well laid out, with a large-diameter speedo (incorporating a trip recorder as well as a total-mileage recorder), rev-counter, fuel gauge and combined water-temperature and oil-pressure gauge. The facia is covered with anti-reflective black leatherette and has a padded roll along the top.

Minor controls consist of neat tumbler switches and push-pull cables. A pull starter control is still used, in addition to a key ignition switch. Surely it's time B.M.C. swung over to the modern key-starter device for all their models!

The choke control for the twin 1⅛in. SU carbies has an excellent "twist-and-lock" action which makes warming-up a simple affair. The winking traffic indicator control is mounted in the centre of the dash which is a two-way tumbler switch which I found difficult to locate in broad daylight, let alone at night. An illuminated switch or a steering-column stalk (or even a steering-wheel boss switch) would have been preferable.

The test car had an electric cigar lighter and an excellent, fully tran-sistorised radio, built-in at the left end of the dash. Reception was exceptional, and the instant performance from the transistorised receiver (no "warming-up" period is required) was most convenient; at speed, however, the rather high noise level of the car (particularly with hardtop fitted) made listening difficult.

Lively, Yet Docile

Whatever complaints I may have had about the details of the car, I

MG MIDGET GT

BMC plays more performance games with a possible, even probable eye on future production.

BY JOHN BLUNSDEN

ALTHOUGH THERE IS NO SIGN of the MG Car Company revoking its decision not to directly support motor racing, there has at least been a move in the right direction this year. Dick Jacobs, until his Le Mans accident in 1955 a works MG driver, and since then an entrant of Abingdon-built cars in his own right, is fielding a team of factory built and owned Grand Touring MG Midgets in a number of British events. At present his racing program is a modest one, for 1962 is being used as a trial period for the new cars, with the prospect of more interesting things to come.

The story of the GT Midgets really starts well over a year ago, when Jacobs was looking for a car to replace his team of MGA Twin-cams which he had recently sold after two quite successful years on the circuits. The Midget seemed the logical answer, so, armed with a few ideas on how to improve the production model, he went to talk to John Thornley ("Mr. MG") and Sid Enever, the company's engine expert.

Both men were receptive to Jacobs' suggestions, but rather than modify existing production cars, and possibly run into homologation problems, they said they would prefer the factory to build a team of special cars incorporating Jacobs' ideas. These would remain the property of the works, but would be loaned to Jacobs, who would look after

their maintenance and racing program, from his garage at Woodford, Essex – about 20 miles east of London. (It may come as no surprise to hear that Dick holds a thriving MG dealership!)

Three cars have been built, two to race and the third to be held as a spare. The drivers are Alan Foster (who was in the MGA Twin-cam team) and Andrew Hedges – a successful saloon-car driver. The cars' competition debut was on Whit Monday, when Foster managed to mix it with some Lotus 23s for a couple of laps of Goodwood before power inevitably told, while his lap time of 1 minute 42 seconds was only about 9 second outside last year's Formula Junior record for the Sussex circuit.

This was a remarkable achievement for a car which is so close to standard as to be scarcely believable. Indeed, these GT babies could be cited as excellent examples of how to achieve so much with so little.

Even the bodywork is basically standard. The attractive shape has been obtained by taking the production shell and fitting to it an elongated nose section (at Thornley's suggestion, John being a great believer in maximum possible air penetration) and adding an extended version of the optional production hardtop. The normal hardtop has been used as a mould from the top of the screen to well behind the trailing edge of the doors, and a "fast back" section, to Jacobs' specification, has been blended into it. There is a slight lip just above the top of the rear screen, and this is the meeting point of the "old" and the "new". The front screen has also been given more rake.

If Dick Jacobs warrants any criticism as a race entrant it is that he is over-cautious in his approach to FIA regulations. He always errs on the safe side, and this fact, combined with the immaculate condition in which he maintains and presents his cars, probably explains why he causes less drama than most other entrants at pre-race scrutineering. It also explains the unsensational mechanical specification of his new team cars.

Contrary to many reports following their first appearance, the GT Midgets were not equipped with highly-tuned Formula Junior 1,100 cc engines, or even 997s; they had the normal BMC 'A' series 948 cc block, bored out to the maximum permissible 40 thou, which gives 979 cc.

Apart from the cylinder dimensions, I suppose you could say that the power unit is modified to Formula Junior standard, although the power and torque curves suggest that the timing is not as extreme as it could be.

Very clean in rear treatment, the steel-bodied coupe has no trunk lid. General construction and detail finish make for suspicions about production; a bit too neat for prototypes.

The interior is stark, typically GT, but a lot cleaner than the Sebring Sprite tested in our Sept. issue. Note 8000 tach.

The very effective dual-choke Weber carburetor is mounted on a special manifold, and of course is used without air filters, while the four-branch exhaust blends into a standard silencer. Naturally, the combustion chambers and porting have been attended to, but here again the modifications are not as radical as on some tuned BMC 'A' series engines. No power figures have been issued for the Midget engines, but at a guess I would put the peak output at no more than 80 horsepower.

One modest concession to high performance is a close-ratio gearbox, but the standard 4.875 to 1 axle is used. The Borg and Beck clutch is also basically standard, but with the usual competition center plate. Lockheed disc brakes are fitted at the front, and normal drums at the rear — a set-up which is already marketed widely for the Sebring Sprites, as indeed are the wire wheels. Ironically, these items have produced more homologation problems than any other part of the car — it seems that although they had been cleared for the Sprite, the necessary paper work had not been completed in respect to the MG Midget. This was hastily rectified!

There are just a few minor suspension alterations, including higher rate coil springs and an anti-sway bar at the front. The standard Armstrong front shock absorbers are used, with competition settings, while adjustable Armstrongs are fitted at the back in conjunction with the normal quarter-elliptic springs. The production radiator is retained without cooling fan, but an oil cooler has been added at the front.

The combination of the longer nose, the more sloping screen, and the fast back has greatly improved air-flow according to tests in the wind tunnel, and this is obviously an important contribution to the car's greatly improved performance. Even better penetration should result when the headlamps are recessed behind plastic shields blending into the general body line.

The side screens are fixed permanently to the doors on the racing Midgets, although they incorporate the usual sliding panels. The interior is devoid of unnecessary trimming, the only luxury being the occasional piece of sorbo padding to protect the drivers' legs. But even so, there is none of the cannibalized look that we find in so many competition versions of production cars, while the interior finish is almost as good as the outside. The first two cars have been finished in a tasteful shade of mid-green, while the third car is painted blue.

Even utilizing such a high proportion of normal production parts, the construction of the team cars has quite a costly project. It is obviously being looked upon as a

long-term venture, with some of the most significant developments taking place in that immaculate engine compartment. The 997 cc Formula Junior engine has been built in sufficient quantity to cause no homologation problems, but the real sting of the GT Midgets will be felt when they carry the 1,100 cc unit, with the eight-port head — a development which is imminent. Then they should really fly, and what delectable little GT cars they will be!

A lot of people have been asking the inevitable question: "When will a production version be announced?" The quick answer to that one is "Who knows — maybe never!" At present this is strictly a competition endeavor, but those optimists who are hoping to buy a replica from a dealer's showroom may be heartened by the thought that the MGA appeared first of all as a racing prototype. But in case they get too excited, they might also remember that the gap between the first prototype and the production version was several years!

Nevertheless, enthusiasts Jacobs, Thornley and Enever have shown us that there is quite a lot of scope for development in that innocent little sports car that goes under the name MG Midget.

Anyone interested in following it up?

Spare tire and large gas tank occupy the majority of space in the aft section. Visibility is good through large rear window.

One-liter engine is probably the same as that in the Sebring Sprite, output near 80 hp. Note Weber, four-branch exhaust.

"OUR JACK" with his latest creation—a real wolf in sheep's clothing (the MG-Climax, not J. Brabham).

Ex-champ has devised an engine swap that turns new MG Midget into a giant-killer, writes David Phipps after a private tryout

MG-CLIMAX FROM BRABHAM

CLIMAX fits neatly in Midget's bay, is 40lb. lighter than normal unit but gives 80 percent more power. Theoretical maximum is 112 m.p.h.

JACK BRABHAM has done it again! First the Herald-Climax, now a Climax-engined Midget—and this time the results are even more amazing.

In bare figures, an 80 percent power boost improves acceleration from 0 to 50 m.p.h. by over 100 percent, halves the time required to go from 40 to 60 m.p.h. in top gear, and raises maximum speed by 25 m.p.h. On the road it turns a pleasant, good-handling but not particularly lively little roadster into a real high-performance sports car.

For all its implications, the Brabham conversion for the Midget is remarkably simple. It consists merely of replacing the standard engine and clutch with a 1216c.c. Coventry-Climax FWE unit and a special 7½-inch clutch. (Surprising as it may seem, the Climax engine is 40lb. lighter than the B.M.C. unit, with beneficial effects on weight distribution.) An 8000 r.p.m. tachometer is also supplied, and total price of the conversion, fitted, is £360stg.

The test car also had disc brakes on the front wheels and an anti-roll bar — both of which are recommended optional extras — and 5.60 by 13in. Dunlop B7 tyres, the latter mainly to ensure safety at speeds in excess of 100 m.p.h.

Naturally, the conversion is also applicable to the Midget's twin brother, the Austin-Healey Sprite, in both Mark I and Mark II form. In fact, the most obvious application of this conversion would seem to be a used Mark I Sprite, which could probably be obtained and converted at a total cost only £100 above that of a new Midget or Mark II Sprite.

The Climax FWE, a four-cylinder, single-overhead-camshaft unit, has a very good reputation following years of extremely successful racing. As fitted to the Midget, it produces 83 b.h.p. at 6400 revs, yet is even more flexible than the standard MG engine. It also compares very favorably in terms of fuel economy, starts easily from cold, warms up quickly and shows no sign of temperament in city traffic.

On the Road

As can be imagined, with the free-revving Climax engine allied to the agility of the Midget, this is a most enjoyable car to drive — as I found when Jack lent me one for a tryout.

Seating position is good, and pedals, instruments and minor controls are all well placed. The test car's appearance was enhanced by the fitting of a three-spoke wood-rim steering-wheel. Even with the top up, visibility is quite good for a car of this type.

The great thing about the Climax-engined Midget is that it can take advantage of the smallest gaps to pass slow-moving traffic. All its responses are immediate: it goes where it is pointed, and it does so quickly. This applies even if top gear is used most of the time.

The keen driver is not likely to stay permanently in top, however, for the gearshift is very pleasant, and the standard gear ratios seem absolutely ideal for the Climax engine, giving maximum speeds (at 7000 r.p.m.) of 35 m.p.h. in first, 58 in second and 81 in third.

On paper, 7000 r.p.m. in top represents 112 m.p.h., which the car might reach under favorable conditions in hardtop form. The modified brakes are fully able to cope with the performance and seem immune to fade in normal use. The lights are adequate for fast night driving — but the low build of the car causes some oncoming drivers to object to the dipped beams.

It says much for the basic Midget that the Climax-engined version will run straight and true at over 90 m.p.h. in very windy weather, and that the roadholding is in no way

(Continued on page 43)

JOHN BOLSTER

tests

The ⬡MG⬡ MIDGET

THE M.G. Midget is a more luxurious version of the Austin-Healey Sprite or, if you prefer it, the Sprite is a simplified Midget. Both cars are identical mechanically, and they have recently been endowed with the latest long-stroke 1,098 c.c. variation of the B.M.C. A-series engine. This unit has more "punch" than its 948 c.c. predecessor, producing its maximum torque at 2,500 r.p.m. 60 b.h.p. (s.a.e.) is developed at 5,750 r.p.m., as compared with the 47.5 b.h.p. of the earlier models.

The well-known power unit has pushrod-operated valves in a cast-iron head. Twin SU carburetters are fitted and the compression ratio is 8.9 to 1. The single dry plate clutch, four-speed gearbox, and open propeller shaft are entirely conventional. A punt-type welded steel structure forms the chassis and is the basis of the body. Helical springs constitute the suspension medium in front, and at the rear a pair of quarter-elliptic springs are attached beneath the axle with radius arms above. Disc brakes are employed in front with drums behind, and the steering is by rack and pinion.

A pleasing shape has been chosen for the body, combining Italian angularity with some traditional curves. One must admit that the result is attractive, and there is plenty of room for two large people. By retaining detachable sidescreens, it has been possible to hollow out the doors, to the great advantage of the driver and passenger who gain useful elbow room in consequence. The boot is largely occupied by the spare wheel but there is some useful luggage space behind the seats. This is covered by a cushion, presumably for the carriage of a baby or a dog.

The hood is very neat indeed, being easy to erect and remaining in place at maximum speed, though it does flap a little. The sidescreens have sliding panels which do not tend to creep. A useful array of proper round instruments includes a rev. counter.

Although the seats are quite comfortable, one could do with even better lateral location and a bit more support for the thighs. A pleasant driving position, giving a good all-round view, includes well-placed pedals and a central gear lever that can be reached without stretching. Pleasantly smooth except for one slight period, the engine is flexible,

and although the exhaust has a healthy note it is by no means noisy.

Over average road surfaces, the little machine gives a comfortable ride and does not tend to pitch. There is some roll, and a tendency to oversteer is noticeable. During normal driving, the steering feels light and precise. On a racing circuit, the car at first feels rather "soft" but with practice quite fast cornering may be enjoyed. Harder damper settings and an anti-roll bar would be advisable for competition work, but the standard settings are a good compromise for fairly fast touring.

The maximum speed is just under 90 m.p.h. and the engine seems content to cruise at almost any figure within its range. It revs freely, and so although the gear ratios are not particularly close, a useful 70 m.p.h. may be exceeded on third speed and 50 m.p.h. comes up on second. To cover the standing quarter-mile in less than 20 seconds must be regarded as satisfactory for a vehicle of this size and price.

Even when driven hard, the Midget returns a praiseworthy 35 m.p.g. Though the hood gives good protection, the best way to enjoy this car is to get out into the country with the top down. The very efficient heater still keeps the feet warm, and the little machine runs with great ease at quite high cruising speeds.

The easy gear change encourages one to use third speed a good deal, though the flexibility on top is perfectly normal by four-cylinder standards.

The brakes are very good indeed, taking no objection to continuous hard use. The song of the exhaust is always present, reaching quite an inspiring note at full speed, but it does not crackle or boom on the overrun, nor does it seem to attract unwelcome attention.

The appearance of the Midget, on the other hand, certainly draws some admiring glances. Although the general impression is of a sporting nature, the comfort and refinement of the interior are not inferior to normal saloon standards. The whole purpose of the car is to provide reliable everyday transportation while giving the driver the pleasure of handling a lively, responsive machine. Obviously, a sporting two-seater of this type can easily be developed much further if extreme performance is the aim, but we are dealing at present with the production Midget in standard tune.

The small M.G. is a sports car of conservative design. Yet, it has been evolved to a point where it does its job very well and goes on doing it. Of pleasant appearance and with many practical features, it represents good value for money and offers low running costs.

ACCELERATION GRAPH

SPECIFICATION AND PERFORMANCE DATA

Car Tested: M.G. Midget sports two-seater, price £598 13s. 9d., extra: Heater £14 10s., including P.T.

Engine: Four cylinders, 64.58 mm. x 83.72 mm. (1,098 c.c.). Pushrod operated overhead valves. 8.9 to 1 compression ratio. 60 b.h.p. at 5,750 r.p.m. Twin SU carburetters. Lucas coil and distributor.

Transmission: Single dry plate clutch, four-speed gearbox with synchromesh on upper three gears and short central lever, ratios 4.22, 5.73, 8.09, and 13.50 to 1. Open propeller shaft. Hypoid rear axle.

Chassis: Punt-type chassis in unit with steel body. Independent front suspension by wishbones and helical springs. Rack and pinion steering. Rigid rear axle on quarter-elliptic springs with radius arms. Lever-type dampers all round. Lockheed hydraulic brakes with front discs and rear drums. Bolt-on disc wheels fitted 5.20-13 ins. tyres.

Equipment: 12 volt lighting and starting. Speedometer. Revolution counter. Oil pressure, water temperature and fuel gauges. Windscreen wipers and washers. Flashing direction indicators. Heater (extra).

Dimensions: Wheelbase 6 ft. 8 ins. Track (front) 3 ft. 9¼ ins. (rear) 3 ft. 8¼ ins. Overall length 11 ft. 5¼ ins. Width 4 ft. 5 ins. Turning circle 32 ft. Weight 13 cwt.

Performance: Maximum speed 89 m.p.h. Speeds in gears: 3rd, 72 m.p.h.; 2nd, 51 m.p.h.; 1st, 32.5 m.p.h. Standing quarter-mile 19.8 secs. Acceleration: 0-30 m.p.h., 4.4 secs.; 0-50 m.p.h., 9.5 secs.; 0-60 m.p.h., 16.4 secs.

Fuel Consumption: 35 m.p.g.

AUTOSPORT, JULY 26, 1963

THE details of the M.G. Midget, and its companion Austin-Healey Sprite model, are well known. This is an entirely conventional small sports car, with a front engine and rear drive.

The latest Midget has a long-stroke engine of 1,098 c.c. The subject of the current test is a 1961 Midget, which originally had a 950 c.c. unit. This has been bored out to 1,080 c.c. by Speedwell but retains the less exaggerated stroke dimension of the earlier engine. In consequence, it is more suitable for sustained operation at high revolutions, the stroke being 76.2 mm. against 83.7 mm.

This particular machine is tuned almost up to Formula Junior standards, but retains an acceptable degree of flexi-

the car as well as reducing drag. The tail section of the current Midget is not well streamlined and even better results can be obtained with an early Sprite shell.

The performance of this little car on the road is very fine indeed. Although the engine is quite flexible, it is not at its best below 4,000 r.p.m., at which speed one is really in business. The power is well maintained up to 7,500 r.p.m. and so the effective band is a wide one. I was given permission to touch 8,000 r.p.m. but I obtained the best acceleration by changing up at 7,500 r.p.m., so this figure has been used in quoting the maxima in the gears. At the timed maximum speed of 105.8

an insurance policy. I covered many miles at a genuine 100 m.p.h. and the engine remained smooth and kept perfectly cool. An electric fan was fitted ahead of the radiator.

I was surprised to find that I averaged 26 m.p.g. during the flat-out performance testing. One could certainly rely on 30 m.p.g. at normal road speeds. The oil consumption was moderate and did not rise excessively at sustained high speeds.

I came to the conclusion that Speedwell have all the answers where the small B.M.C. engine is concerned. They can supply speed equipment for quite moderate tuning operations, but for the man who really wants to motor the "Clubman 85" job is the answer. You certainly can't break it, because I've tried! For further particulars, contact Speedwell Centre, Cornwall Avenue, London, N.3.

JOHN BOLSTER tests
A SPEEDWELL MIDGET

SPECIFICATION AND PERFORMANCE DATA

Car Tested: Speedwell M.G. Midget. Price of special engine modifications £250. Bonnet £49 10s. Hard top £37 10s.

Engine: Four-cylinders 67 mm. x 76.2 mm. (1,080 c.c.). Pushrod operated overhead valves in special light alloy head. Compression ratio 11 to 1. 89 b.h.p. at 7,000 r.p.m. Weber twin-choke carburetter. Lucas coil and distributor.

Transmission: Single dry plate clutch, four-speed gearbox with synchromesh on upper three gears and short central lever, ratios 4.22, 5.73, 8.09 and 13.50 to 1. Open propeller shaft. Hypoid rear axle.

Chassis: Standard M.G. chassis with independent front suspension by wishbones and rear axle on quarter-elliptic springs. Disc front brakes and drum rear. Extra: Speedwell anti-roll bar and wire wheels.

Equipment: Standard equipment plus oil temperature gauge and electric radiator fan with thermostatic switch.

Dimensions: Wheelbase 6 ft. 8 ins. Track (front) 3ft. 9¼ ins. (rear) 3 ft. 8¼ ins. Weight 12 cwt. (approx.).

Performance: Maximum speed 105.8 m.p.h. Speeds in gears, 3rd, 81 m.p.h.; 2nd, 55.5 m.p.h.; 1st 33 m.p.h. Standing quarter-mile 16.7 secs. Acceleration: 0-30 m.p.h. 3.2 secs.; 0-50 m.p.h. 7.3 secs.; 0-60 m.p.h. 9.1 secs.; 0-80 m.p.h. 16.4 secs.; 0-100 m.p.h. 40.5 secs.

Fuel Consumption: 26-30 m.p.g.

bility. It has been modified to "Clubman 85" specification, which costs £250 when the customer's existing unit is used as a basis. A special steel crankshaft is dynamically balanced, together with the light flywheel, connecting rods, and flat-top solid-skirt pistons. A new camshaft is employed with special rockers, giving extra leverage and a higher valve lift. The Speedwell light-alloy cylinder head contains large inlet valves and gives a compression ratio of 11 to 1. The manifolds are special and the carburetter is a twin-choke Weber 45 DCOE.

The exhaust system is very carefully tuned for length, and the result of all this is 89 b.h.p. at 7,000 r.p.m. with a maximum torque of 78 lb.-ft. at 5,500 r.p.m. Obviously the potentialities of such a power unit are very great.

A standard chassis is used, but great trouble has been taken to put it together about right. Commercial tolerances in assembly often cause standard Midgets and Sprites to steer badly because the designed suspension geometry is not reproduced. A Speedwell anti-roll bar is fitted in front.

Bodywork modifications include the fitting of a Speedwell "Monza" bonnet. This has central ducting to feed the water radiator, carburetter, and fresh-air intake, while the side ducts look after twin oil radiators. The cost of the "Monza" bonnet is £49 10s. A Speedwell "Clubman" hard top is also fitted, costing £37 10s. These components transform the aerodynamic stability of

m.p.h., the engine was turning at an indicated 7,300 r.p.m.

The fierce acceleration is emphasized by the standing quarter-mile time of 16.7 seconds, during which a speed of 80 m.p.h. was exceeded. Perhaps even more impressive, for so small a car, is the 0-100 m.p.h. time of 40.5 secs. The time taken to reach 80 m.p.h. from a standstill is identical to the 0-60 m.p.h. figure of a standard M.G.

Quite one of the best features of the car is the quiet exhaust system, which allows full acceleration to be used in towns. I did oil up one sparking plug in London but the car is without vice on the open road. Bucket seats, with adjustable back angles, are fitted. However, the adjusting wheel is strategically placed to catch my left funny bone during energetic manoeuvres, so I cannot praise this accessory.

Very remarkable is the stability at the maximum speed. Cars as small as this sometimes need holding at three-figure velocities but with this M.G. a couple of fingers on the wheel suffice. The over-steering tendency of the standard model has gone, the stability in side winds also being greatly improved.

To tune an engine while using the standard bottom end is either to accept rigid limitations or to risk a major blow-up. If you start off with a special crankshaft and a balancing job, you are half-way towards safe revolutions. A light flywheel is easy on the crank and, of course, the oil radiators are as good as

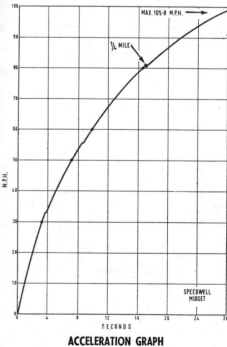

ACCELERATION GRAPH

SHE'S ARRIVED!

THE NEW MG MIDGET

THE CAR THAT *Starts ahead*

SPORTING TRADITION

B.M.C. RESOURCES

ABINGDON CRAFTSMANSHIP

New and exciting, the Midget starts ahead of all rivals — with a great and wonderful *tradition* behind it. It "starts ahead" with a superlative brisk performance through the gears that spells safety every time you overtake; it HUGS the road; it corners FIRMLY; it brakes POSITIVELY in the famous M.G. "Safety Fast" tradition. The M.G. Midget of old swept all before it. The new M.G. Midget starts a winner!

Safety Fast!

WITH A SPORTING APPEAL FROM A SPORTING ANCESTRY

M.G. MIDGET Price £472 plus £197.15.10 P.T. *12 Months'* Warranty and backed by *B.M.C. Service—the most comprehensive in Europe.*

THE M.G. CAR COMPANY LIMITED, SALES DIVISION, COWLEY, OXFORD

London Showrooms: Stratton House, 80 Piccadilly, London, W.1. *Overseas Business:* Nuffield Exports Limited, Cowley, Oxford and 41 Piccadilly, London, W.1

SAFETY '63

SO many irate owners wrote in last time we tested a car from this family (actually it had Austin Healey on the front) and complained of victimisation that we feel bound to delve just a little way into the mystic machinations of whatever sanctum it is that produces SMALL CAR's policy—and explain. You'll have noticed by now that our road tests vary in treatment as well as in length and presentation. We try to work the changes logically.

If the car we're testing is new and little-known we like to give you a fairly detailed rundown on its design and the layout of its controls as well as on the way it behaves.

If it's old and well-known we try to save your time and ours by assuming you have some idea of the basics already. Similarly we fit the test to the car's purpose; a station wagon gets heavy loads and rough farm tracks, a grand tourer a portion of grand touring, a runabout plenty of running about and so on. It doesn't always work out but that's the way we try to do things.

Accordingly a sports car or anything masquerading under that title comes in for fairly specialised appraisal. We reckon the man who buys a sports car buys it because he really likes to drive (how else can he justify paying premium price for less passenger space and less lug-

gage room?). Ergo we spend most of the test space on what we hope is constructive criticism of such vital driving factors as seating, control layout, engine and gearbox performance, roadholding and braking. And when we talk about these things in such a specialised application we apply the very highest standards, naturally.

What niggled the Sprite owners who wrote to us was that we could rave over the handling of, say, a Morris 1100 and then talk about their baby's tail-happiness when obviously we knew as well as they that the Sprite would be the better car to be in in almost any real driving emergency. Our correspond-

ents failed to appreciate that we were speaking relatively.

But to proceed to the Midget. Since we've already dealt with the Sprite in such exhaustive detail (it was the *March* issue, that man at the back) let's stick to the points which differentiate the test car (a) from its kissing-cousin and (b) from earlier models in the same common series. The car we had last time was a sort of interim model: it had the current Mark II body shape but most of the Mark I mechanicals.

Mechanical differences start with the engine, which swells to 1098 cc thanks to the same boring and stroking BMC applied to all the other cars in its non-transverse

A-series line. At 64.6 by 83.7 mm the revised engine is further than ever from being square in the modern manner but BMC seems to make up for that by building in the usual breath reserve along with a stronger crankshaft: you still don't hear of A-engines wearing out, and tuners say they have no more trouble than usual persuading the latest version to spin to a cool 8000 rpm on occasion without harm (we're still talking about fore and aft applications only, by the way).

The next change is in the gearbox, which gets the same excellent Porsche baulk-ring synchromesh setup that transformed the Mini saloons. The box also gets a rubber ▶

coating intended to cut down whine

Modification three affects the anchor department. Lockheed 8-in discs replace the same supplier's 7-in drum brakes on the front wheels, though the drum ditto on the back remain unaltered.

What difference does all this make? Frankly, from our point of view it very nearly transforms the car. Never have we known so few changes to make such an improvement in a model's appeal.

Oddly enough the difference in performance is the one you notice least. The new engine gives nearly 10 bhp more than the old one at identical revs – 55 instead of 46 bhp at 5500 rpm. Acceleration through the gears takes rather less to 40 mph and less again to 60: enough to make a difference to your point-to-point average even though the Spridget is still anything but a winner away from the lights. The precisely calibrated dashboard rev counter (still the only practical reason we can see for buying a Midget and not a Sprite, which has dreadful instruments) has an orange sector from 5500 to 6000 rpm and a red one from there on; in practice we found little point in using the orange band at all except for performance testing and in dealing with the odd cheeky Mini operator, but we fancy the car would have no objection to an occasional excursion into the beyond if you felt you must.

Of far more practical day-to-day use than the extra mechanical urge is the revised gearbox, which above all accounts for the fact that the Spridget is suddenly driveable. It has the same higher and closer ratios that distinguished 948-cc Mark IIs from their pop-eyed and rather depressing ancestors, but without the maddening clunks and graunches that greeted every

attempt at even a semi-smart shift. Instead of a misery it has become a pleasure to change gear really quickly in the latest car. Our only real regret is that first, pleasantly high and eminently usable as it is, should have remained unsynchronised and therefore out of reach to all but the bravest and most skilled. Oh, and it would be nice not to have to put up with all the unaccountable whining and grumbling that still gets past the casing.

The new brakes are an equally welcome improvement from a real driver's point of view. Thrashing older Sprites and Midgets through the lanes you often got the feeling there may be nothing there next time you stepped on the pedal, and occasionally after a really earnest mile or two there wasn't. This time we tried equally hard to make the brakes disappear. We failed.

We didn't think much of the new cockpit arrangements. The so-called crash padding strikes us (ha-ha) as an elaborate practical joke, since it seems to be fastened on *below* the bottom of the dash with skinny little metal brackets that wouldn't stop a stone. The new seats we found better than the old in that they did at least offer some thigh support, but they are still far too upright and far too skimpy. They introduce a new nuisance in the shape of over-flexibility. Standing outside the car we found we could distort the backrests up to six inches with quite mild one-handed pressure, which might give you some idea of the way they writhe.

How does the latest Midget shape up as a sports car, not just in contrast to older models but generally? We found it lively if not paralysingly fast, manageable if not breathtakingly agile, livable if not comfortable, practical if not

perfect. At £599, an acceptable score at least.

We think its styling is dreary to say the least, and we certainly don't think (see pictures) it belongs in what a 100 per cent enthusiast means by the MG genealogy. We disapprove emphatically of a seat position which makes it impossible to use the accepted sports car driving stance – right back with arms straight out and legs almost at full stretch – and which alone is responsible for the spread of that dangerous, rapacious and unfortunately quite incurable automotive disease Spridget Elbow. We laugh at BMC's provision of an optional back seat but sympathise with the reasoning behind its introduction (to keep the insurance companies quiet about third-passenger liability, otherwise a big worry).

On the other hand we approve of the way the car responds to its revised controls – steering always excellent, brakes and gearchange now in line – and we realise that its performance is enough at least to excuse the name sports car if not to justify it. We approve most definitely of the designer's compromise between ride comfort and controllability (in that respect the Midget is almost ideal). We appreciate that the car is safe and reliable even if its handling isn't of the very best (a well-driven Mini will still leave it in the twisty stretches) and we sympathise with the manufacturer in that he has obviously tried hard to provide a satisfactory standard of comfort and convenience in what is after all a grossly unsympathetic configuration.

In all, if social considerations or That Ole Fangio Feeling dictate that you must own a small, cheap sports car then we see no reason why this one shouldn't keep you quiet for a bit. ●

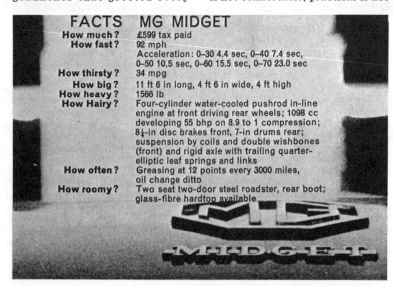

FACTS MG MIDGET

How much?	£599 tax paid
How fast?	92 mph
	Acceleration: 0–30 4.4 sec, 0–40 7.4 sec, 0–50 10.5 sec, 0–60 15.5 sec, 0–70 23.0 sec
How thirsty?	34 mpg
How big?	11 ft 6 in long, 4 ft 6 in wide, 4 ft high
How heavy?	1566 lb
How Hairy?	Four-cylinder water-cooled pushrod in-line engine at front driving rear wheels; 1098 cc developing 55 bhp on 8.9 to 1 compression; 8½-in disc brakes front, 7-in drums rear; suspension by coils and double wishbones (front) and rigid axle with trailing quarter-elliptic leaf springs and links
How often?	Greasing at 12 points every 3000 miles, oil change ditto
How roomy?	Two seat two-door steel roadster, rear boot; glass-fibre hardtop available

Autocar road test 1948

M.G. Midget 1,098 c.c.

YOUNG blood, provided it flows red, has always craved for excitement, and the dream of cutting a dash in a fast, sleek sports car is healthy and virile. Few are fortunate enough to realize their youthful ambition to the full, but the possession of an M.G. Midget is more than a compromise. Far from a thoroughbred by birth, the current Midget still displays the traditional M.G. concept of a sports car, and loses nothing from the doubtfulness of its lineage. It is an exhilarating and predictable car to drive, with a performance that invites one to drive it hard—and to go on driving it.

For over a year now the Midget has been produced with the 1,098 c.c. power unit that was standardized by B.M.C. at last year's Motor Show, and with its two S.U. carburettors and sporting camshaft the peak power developed is 56 b.h.p. net at 5,750 r.p.m. The torque curve has a very flat shape with good bottom-end values and a peak of 62 lb. ft. quite high in the rev. range at 3,250 r.p.m. The only other difference from the car we tested in August 1961 is the adoption of 8·25in. dia. disc brakes for the front wheels and baulk-ring synchromesh in the gearbox.

On the road the extra power can be felt at once (the smaller-engined car developed only 42 b.h.p. net) and the stopwatch showed very worthwhile gains in acceleration. From rest to 80 m.p.h. took 36·9sec, almost 20sec less than before, and the mean maximum speed on a still day was 5 m.p.h. better at 89·5.

There has been no change to the gear ratios, and the indirects feel high but well spaced. First has a maximum of 30 m.p.h., making it a useful traffic ratio, second takes the speed on to 50 m.p.h. and third 70. These speeds are the ultimates corresponding to 6,200 r.p.m. and normally one changes up at around 5,000. The electronic rev counter has an amber warning sector from 5,500 to 6,000, and a red danger zone from 6,000 to 7,000 although valve bounce limited engine speed to a safe 6,300 r.p.m.

Top gear is well matched to the power curve of the engine and the drag of the body (with its extra hardtop), for we were able to go just over peak revs in both directions on the flat. At these speeds engine noise is completely drowned by wind roar and conversation is virtually impossible.

Unusual for a test car, this Midget had covered about 16,000 miles and was over 12 months old. It had obviously

PRICES		£	s	d
Open two-seater		495	0	0
Purchase tax		103	13	9
	Total (in G.B.)	598	13	9
Extras (including P.T.)				
Hardtop with special sidescreens		48	6	8
Heater		14	10	0
Tonneau cover		5	8	9
Rear seat cushion		4	5	0

Autocar road test · No. 1948

Make · M.G. Type · Midget (1,098 c.c.)
(Front engine, rear-wheel drive)

Manufacturers : M.G. Car Company Ltd., Abingdon-on-Thames, Berkshire

Test Conditions

Weather .... Dry, but dank with no wind
Temperature .... 11·0 deg. C (52 deg. F.)
Barometer .... 30·01in. Hg.
Dry concrete and tarmac surfaces.

Weight

Kerb weight (with oil, water and half-full fuel tank)
14·25 cwt (1,596lb-724kg)
Front-rear distribution, per cent F, 51; R, 49
Laden as tested .... 17·25cwt (1,932lb-876kg)

Turning Circles

Between kerbs ....L, 32ft 1in.; R, 31ft 10in.
Between walls .... L, 33ft 5in.; R, 33ft. 2in.
Turns of steering wheel lock to lock .... 2·25

Performance Data

Top gear m.p.h. per 1,000 r.p.m. .... 15·37
Mean piston speed at max. power ... 3,160ft/min
Engine revs. at mean max. speed ...... 5,820 r.p.m.
B.h.p. per ton laden .... 65·0

FUEL AND OIL CONSUMPTION

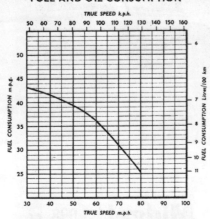

FUEL .... Super Premium Grade
(100-102 octane RM)

Test Distance .... 1,063 miles

Overall Consumption .... 29·1 m.p.g.
(9·8 litres/100 km.)

Normal Range .... 28-35 m.p.g.
(10·1-8·1 litres/100 km.)

OIL: S.A.E.30 ....Consumption 8,000 m.p.g.

MAXIMUM SPEEDS AND ACCELERATION TIMES

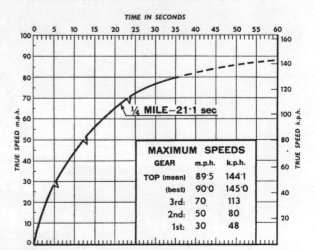

¼ MILE—21·1 sec

MAXIMUM SPEEDS		
GEAR	m.p.h.	k.p.h.
TOP (mean)	89·5	144·1
(best)	90·0	145·0
3rd:	70	113
2nd:	50	80
1st:	30	48

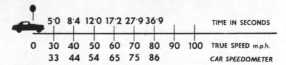

	5·0	8·4	12·0	17·2	27·9	36·9		TIME IN SECONDS
0	30	40	50	60	70	80	90 100	TRUE SPEED m.p.h.
	33	44	54	65	75	86		CAR SPEEDOMETER

Speed range, gear ratios and time in seconds

m.p.h.	Top (4·22)	3rd (5·73)	2nd (8·05)	1st (13·50)
10—30	—	8·1	5·7	4·0
20—40	12·1	8·1	5·5	—
30—50	12·7	8·2	6·5	—
40—60	12·2	9·6	—	—
50—70	15·4	12·7	—	—
60—80	23·2	—	—	—

BRAKES	Pedal load	Retardation	Equiv. distance
(from 30 m.p.h. in neutral)	25lb	0·20g	150ft
	50lb	0·46g	65ft
	75lb	0·85g	35ft
	80lb	1·00g	30·1ft
Handbrake		0·41g	74ft

CLUTCH Pedal load and travel—50lb and 4in.

HILL CLIMBING AT STEADY SPEEDS

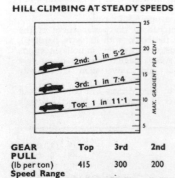

2nd: 1 in 5·2
3rd: 1 in 7·4
Top: 1 in 11·1

GEAR	Top	3rd	2nd
PULL (lb per ton)	415	300	200
Speed Range (m.p.h.)	25–38	32–47	42–56

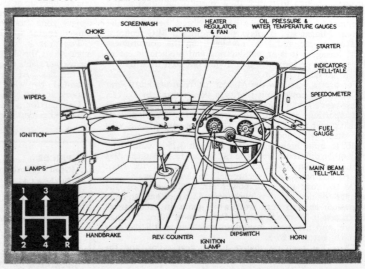

been hard used, but meticulously maintained, and this combination probably put it in nearly the same condition as an average privately owned example. Those sceptics who think that small sports cars are caned to death in a short period would soon be silenced on inspecting this one. The bodywork and interior trim were just as smart as when the car was new, and it was only in a few mechanical details that age was beginning to show.

During the test the starter had to be replaced when it played up and refused to engage its pinion in the flywheel. We missed the starting handle, for which there is no provision, but the Midget required very little impetus to fire when push-started. We also had a little trouble which was probably due to one or other of the carburettor pistons sticking, the symptoms being a sudden loss of power on two cylinders with just as sudden recovery. The exhaust manifold joint, where it meets the down-pipe, tended to leak —a fault common to many other small B.M.C. models.

The car gave indications that it was very nearly due for decarbonizing, for although there was no pinking on premium grade fuel it tended to run on unless we used super. In all other respects, apart from a perceptible whine in the gearbox on the overrun, the Midget was in a very healthy state and obviously good for very many more thousands of miles.

Pulling Power

Comparatively speaking, take-offs from rest felt a little slow and it was not until about 3,000 r.p.m. that the engine really took hold and pulled lustily. By opening the throttle delicately we were able to record some good bottom-end acceleration figures, but it usually pays to hang on to the lower gears and to change down early. The engine had no serious vibration periods, and it seemed to be a much smoother and quieter unit than the older A-series, although it made no secret that it was working hard when called upon to do so.

At the same time as they introduced the larger engine, B.M.C. installed baulk-ring synchromesh on all the A-series gearboxes, and this latest unit is by far the best they have produced. Although first has no synchromesh, a little skill at double-declutching soon makes this a practical ratio for selection on the move, and it always went in first try from rest. Movements of the remote control lever are short and very positive, with a crisp feel that encourages one to make full use of the box.

The disc front brakes were not only more sensitive than the drums they replaced, but proved far more fade resistant from speed. On one or two occasions when braking was deliberately left late from speeds in the upper eighties, the stopping power still turned out to be greater than was required by an appreciable safety margin. Combined with the high-hysteresis Dunlop C41 tyres, the brakes were easily

Carburettor adjustments call for removal of the air cleaners, and the battery is difficult to see into. For the heater fan to blow cold air, the tap on the cylinder head must be turned off by hand

capable of recording 1·0g stops from 30 m.p.h. at only 80lb pedal load, without the benefit of servo assistance.

Nestling alongside the passenger's seat cushion, the handbrake is a little awkward to reach and takes a fair amount of muscle to produce an efficient emergency stop, but it had ample purchase to hold the car fully laden on a 1-in-3 hill. Restarts were not quite possible because of the high first gear, but we did get away without any trouble on 1-in-4.

Much has been written in the past on the handling of the Midget and Sprite with their quick steering, short wheelbase and rear-wheel steering effect, but everyone who drove this car commented on how much safer it felt and how it seemed less prone to dart about at speed. One of the knacks one learns after only a few miles is to relax one's grip on the wheel and let the car find its own path, which it does very accurately. Another factor we found that transformed the handling was to increase the tyre pressure differential from the recommended 2 p.s.i. to 6 p.s.i. between front and rear. This give the car a decided understeer tendency, although some of us still preferred it as it was, when corners could be taken just as fast by a quick

With the passenger's seat right forward there is leg room for one child in the back, but this space is really meant for extra luggage. The cushion is an extra

The soft top is quick and simple to erect, once all the bits have been unpacked; it leaves fewer blind spots than the hardtop

M.G. Midget . . .

tweak on the wheel followed immediately by slight opposite lock correction.

It was more in the straight-line stability that we liked it better without the oversteer. With standard pressures it tended to weave at the slightest provocation when cruising fast, and especially when braking. Our experience with other Midgets has shown that they are also very sensitive to the type of tyres.

Even for acute corners the steering wheel seldom needs more than a wrist movement, and manoeuvres like overtaking hardly require a visible motion of the steering wheel at all; one almost seems to will the car to change course. This high-geared steering meant that when the car was deliberately made to lose adhesion in a corner on a closed test track, corrections could be made speedily and without effort.

On smooth roads the ride comfort is quite acceptable, but rough going really shows up the limitations. Suspension movements are very small, especially at the back, and with two up it is easy to bottom on the bump stops. Tackling the *pavé* was a major feat for the poor little car, which thumped and hopped its way along even at 10 m.p.h. Despite the ordeal, the body felt rigid and solid and nothing rattled except a grease cap from a front hub that came adrift inside the nave plate.

We went through a shallow water trough to test the brakes for wetting, and although they were affected, one application restored them to full efficiency. After a second run the engine cut out due to water short-circuiting the high-tension lead from the unshielded coil.

The road test car came complete with the optional hardtop that costs £48 6s 8d including special side-screens, and we therefore had the choice of three trims. Most of the time the car was run with the glass-fibre roof bolted in place, but during one fine weekend we took it off and tried the plastic-covered canvas hood. Erection is quick, even single-handed, once all the frame tubes and the hood have been unpacked from their various stowage bags, and when it is up and tensioned it makes the car almost as snug inside as does the hardtop.

We encountered heavy rain only with the hardtop on, and this was leak free on the move but tended to let water seep through the side-screen joints when left parked.

Another worthwhile extra we had was the tonneau cover

Left: Door pockets are as big as the doors themselves and make up for the lack of a glove locker. Padded coaming and pile carpets make the inside look quite plush. Right: Hood and frame tools all pack into rattle-free bags, but the spare wheel takes up most of the boot space

that adds another £5 8s 9d. This includes a rail which fits in the hood frame sockets so that the rear compartment can be closed in, and the rest of the cover then clips neatly down behind the seats.

The driver sits with his legs well offset to the right, and even with the seat right back an arms-stretch position is not possible. However, this does not in any way reduce control of the car, and all switches are easy to reach. There is no headlamp flasher; the three-position main lighting switch is close to one's left hand, where it can be used for signalling. The indicator switch is not self-cancelling but there is a bright repeater lamp (that dims when the side-lamps are lit to reduce dazzle) right under the driver's nose. while some disliked this arrangement, others soon became accustomed to it and prefered its positive action.

Although we had the extra cushion for the rear compartment, there is no leg room at all, and this makes it strictly for small children or extra luggage. Getting in and out with the roof on called for some agility, and all too often one catches some clothing on the locating dowel for the door. The doors do not lock, and stealing the car or its contents would be no problem even for the amateur.

The Perspex side-screens have metal frames with rubber sealing strips and panes sliding fore and aft. These must be opened before one can reach in and open the doors, and frost in the runners could be a problem after a night standing out in the depths of winter.

Both bonnet and boot lids have struts that have to be unclipped and fitted into clumsy slots. While that for the engine is not so important, the luggage compartment is opened much more often, usually with one's hands full, and its lid was a continual nuisance. Provided it is of the squashable variety enough luggage for two can be insinuated into the boot, but it must all come out if there should be a puncture.

Over our entire test the fuel consumption averaged 29·1 m.p.g., but this included all the performance measurements and a flat-out trip up M.1. During 500 miles of normal use the overall figure improved to 32·2 m.p.g., but even so the tiny 6-gallon tank meant refuelling stops every 175 miles or so.

The heater, which is yet another extra at £14 10s, impressed us with its high capacity to disgorge streams of really hot air around the foot wells almost as soon as the engine had started from cold. Individual trap doors can be shut for maximum demisting, and the booster fan is not unduly noisy.

Two things about the Midget stand out from our renewed acquaintance with it in its improved form. First, it is a remarkably tough and well-built little car that always feels solid and robust. Second, it is a brisk and nippy machine that has a good margin of safety in all that it does. It has many of the intangible qualities that make a sports car what it is, not the least of which is a natural charm that continually increases one's affection for it. It is the sort of car that is easy to drive well and to have fun with.

Specification : M.G. Midget

ENGINE
Cylinders ...	4-in-line, water cooled
Bore ...	64·58mm (2·54in.)
Stroke ...	83·72mm (3·30in.)
Displacement ...	1,098 c.c. (67 cu. in.)
Valve gear ...	Overhead, pushrods and rockers
Compression ratio	8·9-to-1
Carburettor ...	Two S.U. H.S.2
Fuel pump ...	AC mechanical
Oil filter ...	External, full-flow, renewable element
Max. power ...	56 b.h.p. (net) at 5,750 r.p.m.
Max. torque ...	62 lb. ft. at 3,250 r.p.m.

TRANSMISSION
Clutch ...	6·25in. dia. Borg and Beck s.d.p.
Gearbox ...	Four-speed, synchromesh on 2nd, 3rd and top, central remote control change
Overall ratios ...	Top 4·22, 3rd 5·73, 2nd 8·05, 1st 13·50, Reverse 17·36
Final drive ...	Hypoid bevel, 4·22 to 1

CHASSIS
Construction ...	Integral with steel body

SUSPENSION
Front ...	Independent, coil springs and wishbones, Armstrong lever-arm dampers
Rear ...	Live axle, quarter-elliptic leaf springs, radius arms, Armstrong lever-arm dampers
Steering ...	Rack and pinion, wheel dia., 16in.

BRAKES
Type ...	Lockheed hydraulic, disc front, drum rear
Dimensions ...	F, 8·25in. dia.; R, 7in. dia.; 1·25in. wide shoes
Swept area ...	F, 135 sq. in.; R, 55 sq. in. Total: 190 sq. in. (220 sq. in per ton laden).

WHEELS
Type ...	Pressed steel disc, 4 studs 3·5in. wide rin
Tyres ...	Dunlop C41, tubeless 5·20—13in.

EQUIPMENT
Battery ...	12-volt 43-amp. hr.
Headlamps ...	Sealed beam 40/45-watt
Reversing lamp ...	None
Electric fuses ...	2
Screen wipers ...	Two blade, single speed, self-parking
Screen washer ...	Extra
Interior heater ...	Extra
Safety belts ...	Extra, anchorages provided
Interior trim ...	Leathercloth
Floor covering ...	Carpet
Starting handle ...	No provision
Jack ...	Ratchet pillar
Jacking points ...	One each side in centre of body
Other bodies ...	None

MAINTENANCE
Fuel tank ...	6 Imp. gallons (no reserve)
Cooling system ...	10 pints (plus 1 pint for heater)
Engine sump ...	6·5 pint. Change oil every 6,000 miles; change filter element every 6,000 miles
Gearbox and over-drive ...	2.5 pints SAE 30, no change necessary after first 500 miles
Final drive ...	1·5 pints SAE 90, no change necessary after first 500 miles
Grease ...	12 points every 3,000 miles
Tyre pressures ...	F, 18; R, 20 p.s.i. (normal driving) F, 24; R, 26; p.s.i. (fast driving) F, 18; R, 24 p.s.i. (full load)

Scale: 0·3in. to 1ft.

Cushions uncompressed.

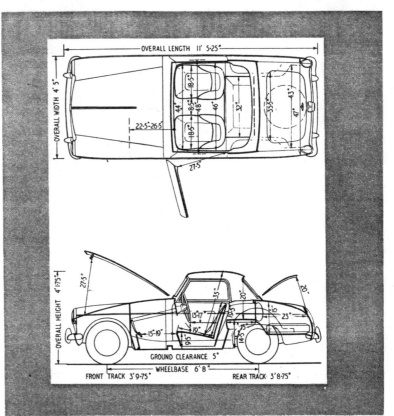

Cars on Test

TAURUS-TUNED M.G. MIDGET 948 c.c.

Engine: As standard B.M.C. 948 c.c. "A" series except Taurus Stage I cylinder head; heavy duty valve springs; twin 1½ in. S.U. carburetters on special Taurus manifold; Taurus sports camshaft; sports coil; B.M.C. competition exhaust system.

Transmission: Four-speed and reverse gearbox with synchromesh on upper three forward ratios. Ratios as standard M.G. Midget.

Brakes: Standard.

Dimensions: Standard.

PERFORMANCE

	m.p.h.			secs.
MAXIMUM SPEED	— 98.2	ACCELERATION	0–30 —	4.4
			0–40 —	7.8
SPEEDS IN GEARS First	— 32.0		0–50 —	10.2
Second	— 54.0		0–60 —	13.6
Third	— 76.0		0–70 —	20.5
			0–80 —	30.6
FUEL CONSUMPTION	36.5 m.p.g.	Standing quarter-mile	—	19.8

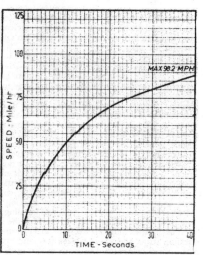

Tuning carried out by: Taurus Performance Tuning Ltd., 14a Thorpe Mews, Cambridge Gardens, Ladbroke Gardens, London, W.10.

CARS
ON TEST

TAURUS-TUNED
M.G. MIDGET
948 c.c.

THE TUNING OF popular sports cars can either result in a car which shows an all-round improvement, or in a car which is certainly faster, yet which is noisy, harsh and intractable. Much depends on the degree of tune which is applied, but much more depends on the manner in which the job is tackled.

Tuning equipment from Taurus Performance Tuning Ltd., of 14a Thorpe Mews, Cambridge Gardens, Ladbroke Grove, London, W.10, has already achieved a reputation worth having from the point of view of reliability and power increase, and although we have come across Mini-Minors which have received the Taurus "treatment" we had not until recently had an opportunity of examining their work on a popular small sports car. We are grateful to Mr. Howard Cohen, of London, N.2, for allowing us to sample his 948 c.c. M.G. Midget.

This well-maintained car, it must be borne in mind, is now more than two years old, and the Midget is no longer produced with this engine size, a replacement having been effected in current models by the 1,098 c.c. B.M.C. "A" series engine. Mr. Cohen's car, however, retains the smaller capacity engine, which in standard form developed some 43 b.h.p. When presented to Taurus for attention, the car had been carefully run in, and had covered 10,000 miles. The Taurus stage I cylinder head was fitted, raising the compression ratio to 10.4 to 1: this head has gas-flowed and polished combustion chambers, the inlet ports opened out and polished and the venturi in the port improved to provide better low-speed torque characteristics. Stronger valve springs are also included. Subsequent modifications included the fitting of twin 1½ in. S.U. carburetters, a Taurus sports camshaft and a sports coil, together with a B.M.C. competition exhaust system. In addition, the car was fitted with Dunlop SP tyres. The cost of the operation was moderate: the Taurus head, including valves and valve springs, costs £28 fitted at the works; twin 1½ in. S.U. carburettors on a new manifold cost £30 10s. fitted, while the camshaft and fitting charges add a further £16 to this total.

The result is a small sports car of modest engine capacity and thirst for fuel with a performance considerably in excess of the standard. In fact, the Midget's performance is, incidentally, rather better than that of the standard 1,098 c.c. model. It remains tractable and pleasant to drive, although traffic driving is somewhat complicated by the competition clutch which has been fitted to the car. This, naturally, grips extremely well, however, and is entirely capable of dealing with the additional power provided by the engine modifications. Throughout the test period, the car started easily whether hot or cold, and provided ample pulling power from cold. Idling was reliable, if a trifle lumpy, but this characteristic is to be expected when a high compression ratio is employed.

Once warm, the engine remains pleasantly smooth, and low-speed power is good. Thick traffic brings no problems with regard to oiling plugs, and the only point which distinguishes the car from standard is a rather loud exhaust note. Free-revving is a notable characteristic of the power unit, which will nevertheless pull away cleanly in top gear from as low as 1,200 r.p.m. There are no vibrations, and the engine remains mechanically quiet.

Despite its pleasant flexibility, it is at crankshaft speeds in excess of 3,500 r.p.m. that the modifications really begin to take effect. Above this speed, one can definitely feel the engine taking hold, and things begin to happen. Speeds in excess of 80 m.p.h. can be maintained for long periods with no sign of dropping oil pressure or rise in water temperature, during the performance testing we detected a slight "fluffing" at above 6,000 r.p.m.—we were asked not to exceed 6,500 r.p.m.—while, on the over-run, an unpleasant transmission vibration occurred at about 4,000 r.p.m.

It proved impossible to record a maximum speed figure on our usual two-way basis, since the hood refused to stay put at high speed when running into the prevailing wind. The car was clearly faster with the hood in position than without it, and after several attempts the project was abandoned after we had obtained the impressive one-way speed of just over 98 m.p.h. The car's acceleration was notably better than the standard 1,098 c.c. Austin-Healey Sprite—the Sprite and Midget are in all important respects identical—road-tested earlier by CARS ILLUSTRATED, the report on which was published in our November, 1963 issue. The Taurus-tuned 948 c.c. car was timed at 19.8 secs. for the standing quarter mile, compared with 19.9 secs. for the 1,098 c.c. Sprite. The Midget, however, required only 13.6 secs. to reach 60 m.p.h. from rest, compared with the Sprite's time of 15.1 secs., and acceleration times to other speeds show a similar improvement in comparison.

Fuel consumption on the Midget was scarcely affected by the increase in performance. An overall figure of 36.5 m.p.g. was obtained over the test mileage, which included driving in thick traffic as well as fast, open-road motoring.

MG MIDGET

(Continued from page 10)

roll when cornering, even at low speeds. The live rear axle is mounted on quarter-elliptic springs and located by trailing links. Body roll promotes rear-wheel "steering," and the car is prone to roll-oversteer from quite low speeds—yet fast cornering is easy enough.

The engine is incredibly willing, and if you make full use of the gearbox the car will cover the ground at a surprising pace. The engine sounds busy at most speeds, and there is a great deal of fan noise at high revs. Low revs produce little power, but the Midget will trickle along without snatch in top gear, provided the throttle opening is kept constant. Strong acceleration, however, demands a change-down—as befits a sports car.

With its sporty camshaft, the A Series engine (as fitted to the Midget) goes in three "stages." It starts to "go" at 1500 revs, takes another bite at 3500, and really comes to life at 5000.

The rev-counter has a "technicolor" section from 5000 to 7000 r.p.m., the final scarlet strip ending at 7000, and the engine is very willing to enter the red in the indirect ratios.

Interior noise is understandably high (particularly with the hardtop) when revs are used freely and there is a surprising amount of structure vibration, especially on the overrun.

No pinging or running-on was apparent during the test, but 100 octane fuel is very desirable with the 9-to-1 compression ratio. Warming-up is rather a slow process, and during recent icy spells the car required about three miles of gentle driving before the water-temperature gauge needle would start to creep up. The car was also prone to carburettor icing during warming-up periods.

Springing is firm, in true sports-car fashion. Although the hardtop doesn't leave much headroom, the suspension is so efficient that my head never made contact with the ceiling, even on bumpy roads.

The drum brakes are well up to the performance, and no fading could be detected at fast road speeds. Pedal pressures are light and the braking action progressive (2 l.s. front, and leading/trailing rear).

The floor-mounted handbrake is not equipped with the traditional MG "fly-off" action, which is a pity. Sited on the left-hand side of the propeller-shaft tunnel, it is also capable of crushing the passenger's fingers if they happen to be in the vicinity when the brake is applied — and with the low seats this could easily happen.

Taken all-round, we found this latest MG to be a fast, non-tricky sports car that could be used for all types of motoring, from fast touring to shopping. Easy to drive and easy on the eye, it is the fastest MG Midget yet — and the easiest to service.

It can also be transformed into a worthwhile competition machine for a relatively modest outlay. Plenty of conversion kits are available in Britain that will raise its maximum speed to 100 m.p.h. or more. Who would have believed, only a few years ago, that such performance could be extracted from a mass-produced car with 948c.c., pushrod-operated overhead-valve engine?

The only catch, so far as you're concerned, is that the new Midget and Sprite won't reach Australia for many months yet.

When they do arrive, I am tipping that it will be in C.K.D. form, for local assembly — which would mean that the Mark II Sprite should cost no more than your present model, while the MG Midget should sell for about £40 more. ● ● ●

" Splendid controllability, good performance . . . make the Midget fun . . . a sports car primarily for sport . . ."

Number 20
MOTOR TESTED
2040 MILES

PRICE
£515 plus purchase tax of £107 17s. 1d. equals £622 17s. 1d.

M.G. MIDGET Mk II

How they run . . .

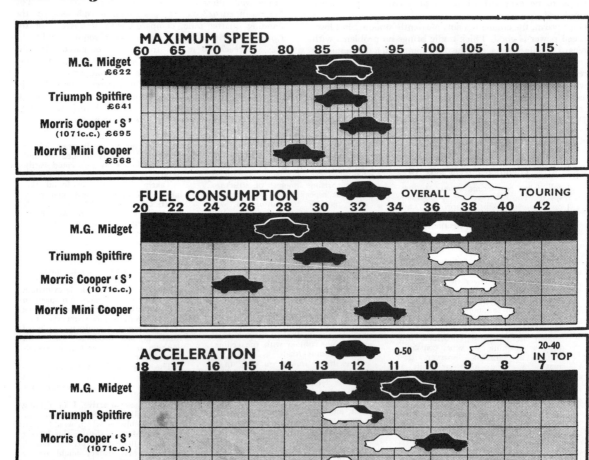

ONE attraction of a small sports car like the Midget is its easy adaptability to the weather. Performance and handling are big considerations, and when the same car can offer all, so much the better. The Midget, and the Sprite before it, have always been praised for their handling, particularly for the accuracy and sensitive feel in the steering. Criticism often aimed at the Mk. I Sprite (effectively the Mark 0 Midget) was that its performance did not match its looks.

The Mark I Midget changed a lot of that, especially when the 1,098 c.c. engine came along; and now the Mark II car

has found a little more power still at slightly higher revs; enough to improve the 0–60 m.p.h. time from 16·6 to 14·9 sec. (compared with the 1100 Sprite we tested). In top gear the 20–40 time is slightly worse, the 30–50 about the same while 40–60 times and beyond are distinctly better, emphasizing the raised power curve due to larger inlet valves and revised cylinder head. Although the performance figures deny it, this car does not feel any less tractable and it is quite content to potter gently.

These, however, are not the biggest changes. Wind-up windows, lockable doors and a heater are held by the early Sprite generation to detract from the original fresh air sports character. Such objection to progress is quite unfounded; the changes widen the potential market of the Midget to include many differing ages and mentalities, and either sex. The original enthusiast, probably single (there is room for little more than a portable cot behind the seats), will like the improvement in cornering stability given by semi-elliptic instead of quarter leaf springs at the rear.

Splendid controllability, good performance and nice lines make the Midget fun, and it has room for a reasonable amount of luggage behind the seats and in the boot. Big people will

Even with the hood down, wind-up windows and a big screen give plenty of protection from cold winds. The front grille distinguishes the Midget from its Austin-Healey Sprite twin.

find it a difficult fit, and knees splayed round the steering wheel will foul the window winder; the space now occupied by the window mechanism has removed the door pocket space (which previously provided extra elbow room) to cramp the tall man still further.

If you still buy a sports car primarily for sport the Midget has plenty of virtues to counteract these shortcomings.

Performance

SPORTS cars are not really meant to be driven very gently in top, but there are times when there is nothing pleasanter than pottering along, hood down, with little noise; in such moods the Midget, at around 20 m.p.h., is quite happy and can still accelerate without changing down. In top gear, 20–30 in 6·7 sec. is 0·3 sec. longer than the 50–60 time and the fastest 20 m.p.h. gap is from 30–50 m.p.h. (about 2,000–3,000 r.p.m.) emphasizing that maximum torque (at 3,250 r.p.m.) appears considerably higher in the speed range than for a family saloon.

Acceleration through the gears is good, with 0–50 m.p.h. taking only 9·9 sec., sufficient to beat most family saloons of twice the M.G.'s capacity. Trying too hard in the wet on take-off, it is very easy to get wheelspin with the lightly laden live axle.

continued on next page

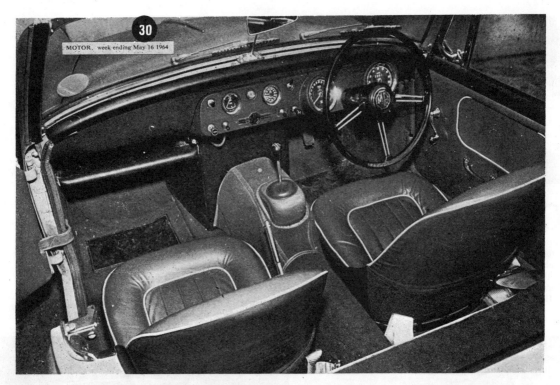

M.G. MIDGET Mk II

Civilized cockpit: well upholstered seats, carpeted floor, and crackle finished facia. Window winding mechanism occupies the former door pockets leaving facia shelf for oddments.

Top speed is now 91·8 m.p.h. which coincides exactly with the beginning of the red sector on the rev counter at 6,000 r.p.m. Taking advantage of down grades puts the revs straight into the orange sector (at 5,500 r.p.m.); a 25-mile spell at around 5,500 r.p.m. on M1 dropped the oil pressure from its customary 55 lb./sq. in. to 40 lb./sq. in.; this was restored to normal after a short distance on ordinary roads but continuous cruising near the maximum speed is probably not advisable and certainly not effortless.

The test car was prone to running on with Premium petrol, so 100 octane grades were used for most of the time. Fuel consumptions have changed a little with the new engine, being at the most 4 m.p.g. worse than the Mk. I Midget. The overall figure of 29·2 m.p.g. represents many miles of sports motoring, but less enthusiastic driving will return figures nearer to our touring fuel consumption of 38·2 m.p.g.

Early morning starts are immediate on full choke, and less than a mile is needed on half choke before the engine is warm enough to pull evenly, although it takes considerably longer for the normal running temperature to come up.

Hill starting is all right up to 1 in 4, but on the 1 in 3 the car staggered to the top on the initial deliberate clutch slip; a long hill, as steep as this, would be too much.

Transmission

WHEN the 948 c.c. engine of the Mk. I was increased to 1,098 c.c. baulk ring synchromesh replaced the earlier not very powerful type, to make it quite unbeatable even during performance testing. The close ratios, unchanged from the previous model, are one of the best sets in production; 6,500 r.p.m. in the gears (halfway up the red sector) gives maxima of 31, 52 and 73·5 m.p.h. with rev drops on the upward changes of 2,600, 1,900 and 1,700 r.p.m. almost the progressive racing ideal.

In the lower ratios there was a certain amount of gear whine, but this seemed more the sound of well-meshed gears with no play. The excellent gearbox is supported by a not particularly light clutch, which always takes up the drive smoothly however quickly the left foot works.

To engage bottom gear smoothly every time at rest, you have first to get almost into second. Partly responsible for this, and wholly responsible for stalling under braking to a standstill, was a dragging clutch, which drops the tickover revs by 200 r.p.m.—enough to stall it with a conventional idling setting.

Handling and Brakes

DESPITE a turning circle of 30 ft. and only 2¼ turns from lock to lock, the Midget steering is unusually light, but there is plenty of feel, noticeable particularly in the wet, as the

The mirror adjusts for height. Larger dials are angled neatly upwards.

Performance

Conditions: Weather: Slight drizzle, misting rain, wind 5–15 m.p.h. (Temperature 39°F, Barometer 29·45 in. Hg.). Surface: Damp tarmacadam. Fuel: 100 octane.

ACCELERATION TIMES

0-30 m.p.h.	..	..	..	4·2 sec.
0-40	..	..	..	6·8
0-50	..	..	..	9·9
0-60	..	..	..	14·9
0-70	..	..	..	21·2
0-80	..	..	..	36·4
Standing quarter mile		..		20·1

On upper ratios				Top	3rd
m.p.h.				sec.	sec.
10-30	..	..	..	15·4	8·6
20-40	..	..	..	12·0	6·6
30-50	..	..	..	10·6	6·5
40-60	..	..	..	11·7	8·2
50-70	..	..	..	13·5	10·3
60-80	..	..	..	18·4	—

The engine is reasonably accessible under the rear-hinged bonnet 1. clutch and brake reservoirs (beneath heater hose) 2. coil 3. starter solenoid 4. distributor 5. dip stick 6. oil filler cap 7. water filler cap 8. windscreen washer bottle.

The boot is large for a small sports car: total volume of cases is 3.1 cu. ft. There is more space behind the bucket seats.

MOTOR   week ending May 16 1964

front end begins to slide if too much lock is put on suddenly. As soon as one becomes accustomed to it, this gives high geared positive control of the best vintage kind, responsive in the extreme but entirely devoid of twitch. The change in rear suspension from quarter to semi-elliptic springs, giving better lateral location of the rear axle, has eliminated the lurch with which previous models were inclined to enter a corner and the consequent feeling of over-sensitivity. Handling is neutral with an easily controllable final breakaway at the back.

The Midget is particularly swervable; some of this responsiveness is due to fairly stiff springing, which can be felt uncomfortably on very bad roads as the car leaps around, but on ordinary roads the latest model is rather less harsh than its predecessor and there is never any feeling of having to hang on to the wheel; one just grips it delicately between the fingers and wills the car round corners; there is little roll,

continued on next page

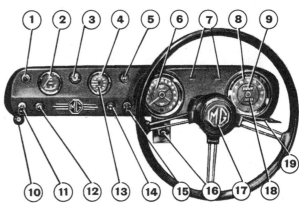

1. windscreen washer 2. petrol gauge 3. ignition starter switch 4. oil pressure gauge 5. lights switch 6. rev counter 7. direction indicator warning lights 8. speedometer 9. trip recorder 10. bonnet release 11. choke 12. wiper switch 13. water temperature gauge 14. panel light switch 15. heater control 16. dip switch (on floor) 17. horn 18. total mileage recorder 19. direction indicators.

MAXIMUM SPEEDS

Mean lap speed banked circuit..	91·8 m.p.h.
Best one way ¼-mile ..	94·7
3rd gear at 6,000 r.p.m. ..	68·0
2nd gear at 6,000 r.p.m. ..	48·0
1st gear at 6,000 r.p.m. ..	29·0
"Maximile" Speed: (Timed quarter mile after 1 mile accelerating from rest)	
Mean	88·0
Best	90·4

HILL CLIMBING

At steady speed		lb./ton
Top	1 in 10·1 ..	Tapley 220
3rd	1 in 6·4 ..	345
2nd	1 in 4·5 ..	490

FUEL CONSUMPTION

Touring (m.p.g. at steady speed midway between 30 m.p.h. and maximum, less 5% allowance for acceleration) ..   .. 38·2
Overall   ..   .. 29·2
                    (=10·3 litres/100 km.)
Tank capacity (maker's figure)   6 gallons

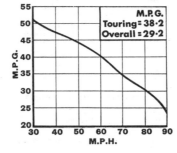

STEERING

Turning circle between kerbs:		ft.
Left		30¼
Right		29¾
Turns of steering wheel from lock to lock		2¼

SPEEDOMETER

30 m.p.h.	..	..	11½% fast
60	..	..	6½% fast
90	..	..	6% fast
Distance recorder	..	..	½% slow

WEIGHT

			cwt.
Kerb weight (unladen with fuel for approximately 50 miles)	..	..	13¾
Front/rear distribution	..	..	53/47
Weight laden as tested	..	..	17½

Test Data: World copyright reserved: no unauthorized reproduction in whole or in part.

BRAKES

Pedal pressure, deceleration and equivalent stopping distance from 30 m.p.h.

lb.	g	ft.
25	·25	120
50	·50	60
75	·76	39½
100	·95	31½
115	·98	30¼
Handbrake	·45	66½

MOTOR week ending May 16 1964

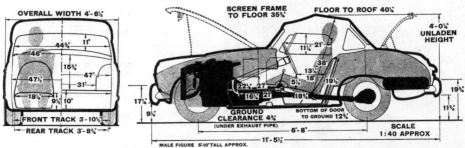

OVERALL WIDTH 4'-6½'

SCREEN FRAME TO FLOOR 35¾"

FLOOR TO ROOF 40½"

4-0¼"
UNLADEN
HEIGHT

FRONT TRACK 3'-10½'

REAR TRACK 3'-8¾'

GROUND CLEARANCE 4¾"
(UNDER EXHAUST PIPE)

BOTTOM OF DOOR
TO GROUND 12¾"

SCALE
1:40 APPROX

MALE FIGURE 5'-10" TALL APPROX.

M.G. MIDGET Mk II

and no tyre squeal to remind passers-by how fast you are going. On very bumpy corners, however, it becomes obvious that the conventional rear axle gives an indifferent sprung/unsprung weight ratio and far more wheel hop than a good independent rear suspension.

Disc brakes, now standard on the front, are effective and fade free, requiring normal pressures (50 lb. for 0·5g. stop) and 115 lb. for the maximum recorded, 0·98g. On the test hill, the handbrake, mounted on the left of the transmission tunnel (and without the traditional M.G. flyoff release) had no trouble with the 1 in 3, and proved very useful as an emergency brake with locked rear wheels recording 0·45g.

Comfort and Control

UNFORTUNATELY, rearward seat adjustment is limited by the front face of the platform over the back axle, so that even the enterprising tall owner will be unable to get himself really comfortable without major body modification or changing the seat profile. For the average man, however, the seats are very comfortable and strike an excellent compromise between a wrap-around side supporting shape and easy access.

The driving position is good for a 5 ft. 10 in. driver, with the wheel far enough away for any necessary arm twirling, although not for a completely straight arm position. A short stubby gear lever, with stiff precise movement, lies just where it is wanted, within a handspan from the wheel rim in top gear. Brake and accelerator pedals are too closely spaced and it is all too easy for a large foot to hit both, although this is ideal for heel and toe use.

However tight you have a fabric hood, it is still inclined to vibrate; the Midget's starts to do so at about 60 m.p.h. but gets little worse at higher speeds so that conversation

is always possible despite any increase in carburetter noise.

The vintage days of a little bit of glass let into a fabric hood for rearward visibility have now disappeared, and current foldable transparent plastic ensures very good vision all round, with no blind spots. At night, headlights on full beam are adequate for the car's performance.

The heating system is very simple—one knob and two flaps. Pull the knob out and the heat is turned off; push in for more air and a final twist (only possible with the knob full in) turns the heater fan on. Flaps on each side of the gearbox tunnel let air onto the legs, or divert it all on to the screen when they are closed. The temperature can be varied only by allowing less hot air in or by turning off the water cock for the summer; but in winter the heater is more than adequate.

Fittings and Furniture

A NEAT crackle black facia has the two main instruments (rev counter and speedometer) canted in towards the driver, and easily visible through the three-spoke wheel. The other two are on the flat part with a combined oil pressure/water temperature and fuel gauges.

Mounted on a vertical rod, the rear view mirror can be adjusted to any position between top and bottom of the screen. Carpets now cover all metal surfaces except the doors, and rubber mats provide extra protection from sharp heels.

A small parcel shelf is situated under the facia (passenger side) and prone to damp, but most luggage will find its way to the rear compartment which will take a quite large suitcase or several small ones; the boot has plenty of room, too, despite the spare wheel.

Lockable doors were supposed to constitute a safety feature, but with the door handle at the rear, it is too easy to undo two hood fasteners and open it. The other disadvantage of this position is that it requires a universally jointed elbow to let yourself out; the passenger's interior lock was particularly stiff. Safety belt anchorages are provided, and the test car had comfortable lap strap and diagonal belts.

MAKE M.G. • MODEL Midget Mk. II • MAKERS M.G. Car Co. Ltd. Abingdon-on-Thames, Berks.

ENGINE

Cylinders	4
Bore and stroke	64·58 mm. × 83·72 mm.
Cubic capacity	1,098 c.c.
Valves	O.h.v. (pushrod)
Compression ratio	9·0 : 1
Carburetter(s)	Twin HS2 S.U.
Fuel pump	S.U. electric
Oil filter	Purolator full flow
Max. power (net)	59 b.h.p. at 5,750 r.p.m.
Max. torque (net)	62 lb. ft. at 3,250 r.p.m.

TRANSMISSION

Clutch	7¼ in. Borg & Beck
Top gear (s/m)	Direct
3rd gear (s/m)	1·36
2nd gear (s/m)	1·91
1st gear	3·20
Reverse	4·11
Final drive	Hypoid bevel 4·22 : 1
M.p.h. at 1,000 r.p.m. in:—	
Top gear	15·3
3rd gear	11·3
2nd gear	8·0
1st gear	4·8

CHASSIS

Construction	Unitary

BRAKES

Type	Lockheed hydraulic
Dimensions	Front 8¼ in. disc; Rear 7 in. drum
Swept friction area	135·28 sq. in.

SUSPENSION AND STEERING

Front	Coil spring with lower wishbone
Rear	Semi-elliptic leaf springs
Shock absorbers:	
Front	Armstrong lever arm as upper suspension link
Rear	Armstrong lever arm
Steering gear	Rack and pinion
Tyres	5·20—13

COACHWORK AND EQUIPMENT

Starting handle	No
Jack	Side lift
Jacking points	Door sill panel
Battery	Lucas 43 amp.-hr. at 20 hr. rate
No. of electrical fuses	Two (and two spares)

Indicators		Flashers
Screen wipers		Lucas single speed
Screen washers		Tudor manual
Sun visors		None
Locks:		
With ignition key		Doors and boot
With other keys		None
Interior heater		Smiths fresh air—optional
Extras		Heater, hard top, luggage carrier, twin horns, heavy duty tyres, wheel discs, Radiomobile radio
Upholstery		Leathercloth
Floor covering		Pile carpet
Alternative body types		None

MAINTENANCE

Sump		6½ pints S.A.E. 30
Gearbox		2¼ pints S.A.E. 30
Rear axle		1½ pints S.A.E. 90
Steering gear		S.A.E. 90
Cooling system		10 pints (2 drain taps)
Chassis lubrication		Every 3,000 miles to 12 points
Ignition timing		5° b.t.d.c.
Contact breaker gap		·014/·016 in.
Sparking plug type		Champion N5
Sparking plug gap		·024/·026
Tappet clearances (cold)		Inlet ·012 in., Exhaust ·012 in.
Front wheel toe-in		⅛ in.
Castor angle		3°
Tyre pressures:		
Front 18 lb. sq. in.—22 lb.		High speed
Rear 20 lb. sq. in.—24 lb.		

CARS
ON TEST

M.G. MIDGET

MARK TWO

THE small sports car has grown up, and has done so quite suddenly in the past couple of years or so. Those who remember the early cars which bore the name "Midget"—and even those who remember the less distant past when B.M.C.'s first contribution to the small sports car field, the Austin-Healey Sprite, first appeared on the market, would find little except dimensions as points of similarity between those and the current M.G. Midget—the "Mark 2" in the line, which is, of course, similar in all respects to the current Mark 3 Sprite.

The first of the small B.M.C. sports cars, the Sprite, was an admirable machine. Small, economical and lively, with high standards of road-holding, it retained such "traditional" sports car features as detachable side-screens, limited and rather awkwardly-placed luggage accommodation, and was possessed of a performance which, although adequate, nevertheless represented only a relatively slight improvement on its less sporting companions in the one-litre category.

With the introduction of the Mark 2 Midget (and the Mark 3 Sprite) the small sports car embarked on a new era, however. The car is nowadays even more a scaled-down version of its lustier stablemates, and it combines such creature comforts as wind-up windows and much-improved interior trim with a

performance of which many so-called sports cars of much greater engine capacity might well be envious.

The current model has a maximum speed comfortably in excess of 90 m.p.h., and will reach 60 m.p.h. from a standing start in around 13 seconds: a cruising speed in excess of 80 m.p.h. can be enjoyed without stress, while its fuel consumption remains extremely moderate.

The power unit is still basically the B.M.C. "A" series engine, now of 1,098 c.c. The unit has pushrod-operated overhead valves, a three-bearing crankshaft and a cast-iron cylinder head. With a nine to one compression ratio, 59 b.h.p. is developed at 5,750 r.p.m. It is a rather rough engine, but one which has plenty of "punch", and whether hot or cold it is an easy starter. Surprisingly, it is also remarkably flexible, and the top-gear performance is good: maximum torque (62 lb./ft.) is produced at 3,250 r.p.m. No snatch or unpleasantness is experienced at speeds below 20 m.p.h. in top gear, and the car will accelerate steadily from this speed to its maximum without the need for a gearchange. When cold it pulls well, although it takes several miles to reach its normal running temperature. It is extremely free-revving, and will pull maximum revs. in top gear: during our performance testing, the needle of the tachometer entered the "amber" sector of the dial when our best one-way maximum speed was recorded. The engine of the test car showed a strong tendency to "pink" when pulling hard: a change to 100-octane fuel gave no apparent improvement, and the ignition timing was

Under all conditions the car is fully-controllable, and is predictable in its handling qualities. Initial understeer promotes considerable tyre squeal: as the limit of adhesion is reached the rear end breaks away but remains easily under the driver's control. Bumps and other road surface irregularities will cause the back of the car to be thrown off-line with some violence, but the quick, positive steering enables adequate correction to be made.

Disc brakes are fitted to the front wheels, combined with drums at the rear. The brake pedal is light to use and the braking capabilities of the system give plenty of confidence. At no time during the test was any fade or uneven pulling experienced, and firm, all-square stopping power could be employed with confidence on wet and dry roads. Occasionally the front discs produced some squeal when applied firmly.

The test car had covered rather more than 6,000 miles when it came into our hands for test. There were no rattles, and the doors shut well: a further improvement on this model over the earlier car is that the doors now have outside handles, and

Right: Wind-up windows, lockable doors and swivelling quarter-lights are now featured on the Midget, together with revised instrumentation. Below right: Principal engine components and accessories are easily accessible.

suspected, although the engine did not run particularly "hot".

The gearbox is a four-speed and reverse unit, with central floor-mounted gear lever and synchromesh on the upper three ratios only. The ratios are well-spaced, and represent a noticeable improvement on earlier models, while the transmission train is quiet in operation. Only the un-synchronised first gear is rather noisy, especially on the over-run. The clutch is light to operate and in general grips well: ultra-fast gear-changes allow a slight amount of initial slip to be detected as the drive is taken up. The gear lever is precise in operation and has a short movement, although its action, on the test car, was a trifle stiff: in addition the lever possessed an annoying rattle, especially when the engine was pulling hard at high r.p.m.

Front suspension is independent, with wishbones and coil-springs. At the rear, the quarter-elliptic longitudinal leaf springs of earlier models have been replaced by springs of semi-elliptic pattern. The suspension gives a level, firm ride, and while bumps can be felt inside the car, wheel movement is well-controlled and there is a pleasing absence of axle-tramp and, on dry roads, wheel-spin is not easily induced.

can be locked. In addition, wind-up windows, their glasses having a pronounced curvature in the interests of maximum body width, and small, opening quarter-lights are now fitted. The hood is draught-free and is now secured by quick-release clips at the top of the windscreen frame: these work well and are easily and speedily manipulated when the hood is raised or lowered. In its lowered position, the hood is completely detached, and stows, with the hood-sticks, in the boot. When erect, it is fully water-proof and provides a snug interior, while the canvas retains its shape and does not flap, even at the car's maximum speed.

With the hood erect, the Midget is not the easiest car in the world to enter or leave, but once one is aboard there is a generous amount of room. The interior of the car has been given something of a face-lift, and comfortable seats, well-shaped and providing adequate support for driver and passenger, combine with a fully-carpeted and well-laid-out cockpit to provide a comfortable long-distance touring car. Front seat adjustment is limited, however, and tall drivers are less well provided for. As it is, even drivers of average height and build find the steering wheel rather too close to the chest, and additional rearward adjustment of the seat is precluded by the luggage space behind, which supplements the outside boot.

The steering itself is light and direct, with a pleasant precision which gives a good feel of the road through the front wheels and which adds to the enormous fun which driving this lively little car can provide. The wheel has three wire spokes, all of which are fitted in the lower half of the wheel so that, with the front wheels in the "straight ahead" position, the driver has an uninterrupted view of the instruments. The speedometer and rev.-counter, both of which have steady needles, are mounted at an angle so that each faces inwards for maximum visibility. The other instruments—fuel contents, oil pressure

and water temperature gauges—are mounted in the centre of the facia, together with the conveniently-placed, but unlabelled, hand controls for lights, screen-wipers, etc. The pedals are well-placed for heel and toe operation, and the gearlever is placed so as to fall conveniently to hand. Visibility all-round is good, and there is an effective heating and de-misting system. The screen-wipers clear a sufficient area of the windscreen in wet weather, but under some conditions two-speed operation would considerably assist their effectiveness: at high speed the blades tended to lift clear of the screen, with obvious deterioration in visibility.

The principal criterion for a sports car is, of course, its performance. In this direction the Midget by no means disappoints the driver. Its maximum speed, comfortably in excess of 90 m.p.h., puts it among the faster cars in the 1,100 c.c. bracket, and endows the car with a comfortable cruising speed of over 80 m.p.h., at which velocity one has the feeling that the engine is running well within its capabilities. Bearing in mind the extent to which the car is equipped, with carpets, wind-up windows and so on, its acceleration is extremely lively. From a standstill, as we have said, 60 m.p.h. can be reached in thirteen seconds. The engine develops its optimum performance in the middle range, so that only a very slight advantage is obtained by holding an intermediate ratio up to the maximum safe crankshaft speed. The gear ratios are well-spaced for a sporting vehicle, and apart from the stiffness of movement mentioned earlier—possibly a point peculiar to the individual model—the gearbox is very pleasant to use. The roadholding reaches a sufficiently high standard to permit very high average speeds to be maintained from point to point: the car's behaviour is at all times predictable and controllable, aided by the high-geared, pleasant steering, and slides can be deliberately induced and easily controlled.

Economical running has always been a feature of the small B.M.C. sports cars, and the latest Midget is no exception. Its fuel consumption must be regarded as extremely moderate in terms of the performance available, and our overall figure for the test mileage, of little short of 1,000 miles, was exactly 32 m.p.g. Very hard driving, including the taking of performance figures, reduced this figure to 30 m.p.g., and there is no doubt that many owners would improve on both these figures by a considerable margin.

Cars on Test

M.G. MIDGET Mark 2

Engine: Four-cylinder, 64·57 mm. × 83·72 mm. (1,098 c.c.); compression ratio 8·9 : 1; pushrod-operated overhead valves; twin S.U. carburetters; 59 b.h.p. at 5,750 r.p.m.

Transmission: Single dry-plate clutch; four-speed and reverse gearbox with synchromesh on upper three forward ratios and central, floor-mounted gearlever.

Suspension: Front, independent with coil springs, wishbones and lever-type dampers; rear, rigid axle with semi-elliptic leaf springs and lever-type dampers. Tyres: 5·20 × 13.

Brakes: Front, 8¼ in. disc brakes; rear, 7 in. drums.

Dimensions: Overall length, 11 ft. 4 ins.; overall width, 4 ft. 5 ins.; overall height, 4 ft. 2 ins.; turning circle, 32 ft. 2 ins.; dry weight, 14 cwt.

PERFORMANCE

	m.p.h.			secs.
MAXIMUM SPEED	— 97·2	ACCELERATION	0–30 —	4·0
(Mean of 2 ways)	— 95·9		0–40 —	6·6
			0–50 —	8·8
			0–60 —	13·0
			0–70 —	16·5
SPEEDS IN GEARS First	— 30·0		0–80 —	27·0
Second	— 54·0		0–90 —	35·9
Third	— 74·0	Standing quarter-mile	—	19·0

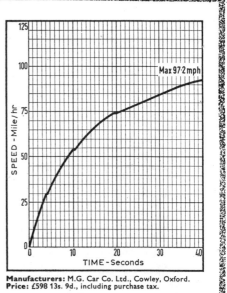

Manufacturers: M.G. Car Co. Ltd., Cowley, Oxford.
Price: £598 13s. 9d., including purchase tax.

MG MIDGET-
Traditionally Yours

One of the most mild, well-mannered of spor ts cars in its range, the Midget is one to suit all tastes and most pockets. There are few come so equipped at the price.

FOLLOWING a preview of the MG Midget, we took our time about putting the car to test. We wanted to live with it a while without being rushed through testing procedures owing to the queue of frustrated would-be Fangios who eagerly grab every new sports car as if it were their own speciality.

And, happily, we are able to report that our time with the revised and renamed Sprite was well worth the patience.

Adding flower to the test of the MG Midget is unnecessary. The basic design has been with us for some length of time and anyone who has been around sports cars knows the value that was always built into the former Sprite.

The big news, though, is in the mechanical departments. BMC, already updating the MGB and preparing to launch the MGC, wasn't ready to let the MG Midget fend for itself just on a change of name — no matter what kind of magic the name MG might conjure in the heart of the purist. So they took the best of everything and built a new car inside the current shell.

For power, engineers plucked out the proven Mini Cooper S unit of 1275 cc. They detuned it with smaller valves and a milder camshaft than used in the Coopers and held the power at 65 bhp at 6000 rpm, giving 72 lb/ft of torque at 3000 rpm. Compression ratio was kept almost the same.

The new engine really turned the little Midget on. Not that it was any slagbox before. With the former 1100 cc motor, the car was still light enough to be able to hold its own with any medium-sized sedan in traffic light derbies, yet it would be completely content to idle along at

very slow speeds without kick-back or fuss.

Not that the 1275 cc version is much different. Helped by a relatively low final drive gear ratio, the Midget is one of the most flexible sports cars around. Geared to run 15.5 mph per 1000 rpm, the 4.22 rear end brings the tachometer red line to 6300 — although the engine is just as happy to spin closer to seven grand — and a top speed of over 100 mph. The Midget would easily pull a higher rear end if you wanted some spirited cruising in the country, but as a dual-purpose sports car the ratio choice currently used is excellent for every need.

Small shortcomings do remain in the Midget design. There is a slightly cramped feeling in the driver's seat — owing to the steering wheel coming back to the driver too far. Actually, this could be turned around to read that the seat doesn't adjust back far enough to allow even a semi-straight armed driving position — and a tallish driver could well find himself experiencing slight pangs of arm fatigue on long journeys.

Whatever the driving position may be to the tall enthusiast, the car is nevertheless comfortable. Passengers have oodles of room for feet and elbows and excellent vision from a normal sitting position. With the side windows wound up and the hood down, there is hardly any wind-blown discomfort, rather a touch of fresh air wafting over the top of the windscreen lightly to fleck the occupants. For a full blast of air and a carefree feeling, simply wind the lot down and hold on to your hat.

The cockpit is fully carpeted, and this extends back to the parcel shelf behind the seats — even when the hood is folded. While overnight bags can be carried on this shelf, any other holiday luggage or parcels will fit easily into the surprisingly-large boot.

Our first impressions of the Midget gave full details of the hood and its new design, so there's

Same styling, different name. Car is very popular and MG insignia should push it to greater heights. Laminated windscreen and headlamp flasher are among optional extras. They should be standard.

Heart of the Midget Mk II is the race-proven four cylinder BMC A-series engine. Of 1275 cc, with pushrod operated ohv, twin SU down-draught carburettors and counter-balanced crank, it develops 65 bhp — reliably, if somewhat noisily.

SPECIFICATIONS

Make .... MG Midget (1275)
Price $2480
Road test mileage .... 348 miles

PERFORMANCE:

Top speed (fastest run) .... 94 mph
Speedometer indication .... 103 mph
Top speed (average) .... 93.7 mph
Rpm at max speed .... 6300 rpm

Speeds in gears   Equivalent rpm

First .... 30 mph   (6300 rpm)
Second .... 52 mph   (6300 rpm)
Third .... 70 mph   (6300 rpm)
Fourth .... 94 mph   (6300 rpm)

Acceleration through the gears:

0-30 mph ...... 4.0 sec   0-60 mph ...... 13.2 sec
0-40 mph ...... 6.3 sec   0-70 mph ...... 19.3 sec
0-50 mph ...... 9.5 sec   0-80 mph ...... 25.7 sec

Acceleration in gears: third   fourth

30-50 mph .... 5.1 sec   7.6 sec
40-60 mph .... 5.5 sec   7.4 sec
50-70 mph .... 6.2 sec   8.3 sec
60-80 mph ....   10.6 sec
70-90 mph ....   12.4 sec

Standing quarter mile:

Fastest run .... 18.9 sec
Average of all runs .... 19.1 sec

Fuel consumption:

Overall for test .... 28 mpg
Normal cruising .... 28-32 mpg
Hardie Ferodo test circuit (1½ mile) —
Fastest lap .... 56.5 sec
Average of all laps .... 57.0 sec

Speedometer error:

Indicated mph: 30   40   50   60   70   80
Actual mph: 27.7 36.7 46.0 54.5 64.2 72.5

CALCULATED DATA:

Mph per 1000 rpm in top gear .... 14.9 mph
Piston speed at max bhp .... 3200 ft/min
Power to weight ratio .... 96 bhp/ton

ENGINE:

Cylinders .... four in line
Bore and stroke .... 70.63 mm by 81.33 mm
Cubic capacity .... 1275 cc
Compression ratio .... 8.8 to 1
Valves .... pushrod overhead
Carburettors .... twin SU HS2
Power .... 65 bhp at 6000 rpm
Torque .... 72 lb/ft at 3000 rpm

TRANSMISSION:

Type .... four speed, syncro 2, 3, 4
Clutch .... 6½ in. dia sdp hydraulic
Gear lever location .... central floor
Overall ratios: 1st 13.5
                2nd 8.4
                3rd 5.7
                4th 4.2
                Final drive .... 4.22 to 1

CHASSIS AND RUNNING GEAR:

Construction .... unitary
Suspension front ..... wishbones, coils, anti-roll bar
Suspension rear .... leaf springs
Shock absorbers .... telescopic hydraulic
Steering type .... rack and pinion
Turns lock to lock 2 1/3
Turning circle .... 32 ft

BRAKES:

Type .... disc front, drum rear
Dimensions .... 8¼ in. dia disc, 7 in. dia drum

DIMENSIONS:

Wheelbase .... 6 ft 8 in.
Track front .... 3 ft 10½ in.
Track rear .... 3 ft 8¾ in.
Fuel tank capacity .... 6 gals
Tyres; size 5.20-13
Ground clearance .... 5 in.
Length .... 11 ft 5 in.
Width .... 4 ft 6½ in.
Height .... 4 ft 1 in.

There's ample room on the shelf for soft baggage as well as the neat-fitting, folded hood. Seat belts anchor to rear side panels of shelf. Note full carpeting over tunnel and rear compartment.

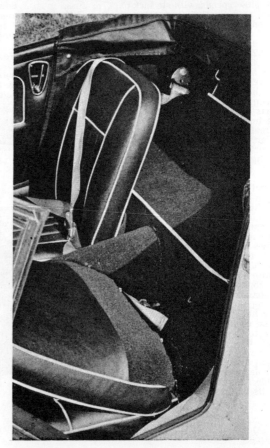

Seats are comfortable but driver's seat won't go back far enough for the tall. Steering wheel is stronger than Sprite model. Safety features are recessed interior door handles, anti-burst locks and roll bar in facia. Note handbrake location.

There are no carpets here, but the large boot is welcome. Spare wheel takes up sizeable portion of available space, but there's still room for plenty of luggage, the softer kind.

little need to go into that again. But we will applaud the company's foresight in supplying a small tonneau cover which clips over and around the folded hood, returning the car to a clean and uncluttered sight.

Handling, apart from the available extra torque, is not seriously changed. The car continues to understeer with regular tyre pressures — which probably keeps the boy-wonders out of potential trouble — but anyone with a bit of thought and driving nous can soon work out a good balance of tyre pressures to bring the car back to some semblance of neutral handling. In fact, it's damned hard to get the car to break the tail loose unless you time your actions and reactions to the split second, on the right corner with the right type of slippery road. Other than going through all of this hard work (you want to try it some-

time) you're probably as safe in the MG Midget as in any other car on the road in its class. On dirt or in the wet, the car is a ball in semi-experienced hands. Almost like a toy. It can literally be chucked around to adopt impossible angles; then brought back into line without turning a hair. A lot of the excellent handling and traction qualities found in the MG Midget can be attributed to the fact that BMC fit radial tyres as standard — a most welcome move.

So, before jumping into the big 'uns and dreaming you're a boy hero right from the start, take a trip in the Midget. It'll give you all the experience you'll want from a sports car, boasts all the features of its big brother and is one hell of a lot of fun to boot.

But at $2480, where have the cheaper sports cars gone? #

Midget is well-balanced from the rear. Locking petrol cap is optional extra. Owners can also specify a luggage carrier, full tonneau cover and anti-roll bar—at extra cost on an already expensive car.

AUTOCAR, 13 May 1966

M.G. M-Type (1929-32)

M.G. J2 (1932-34)

A Comparative Analysis of Midgets 1929 to 1965

MIDGETS have been made continuously since the introduction of the M-Type in 1929, with the exception of the war years and the later '50s. All these Midgets have been astonishingly good value for money achieved as the result of the ingenuity of building a small sports car from slightly modified production saloon parts. Value, however, in the eyes of some ceased with the TF, in the eyes of others with the TC, and in the eyes of a few with the disappearance of the overhead cam, when the PB was discontinued in 1936. The proof of the pudding, however, has been in the eating. It is interesting to note that, with the exception of the P-types, sales figures from one series to another have always increased. There will, it seems, always be a generation hungry for a sports version of Morris's bread-and-butter line.

Here an attempt is made to present a comparative analysis of performance and quality in terms of value, of all Midgets, with the exception of series C, D, Q and R. Taking a pound (£1) in 1932 to be worth 20 shillings, the Westminster Bank Ltd. have kindly supplied the devaluation figures between then and now, the final figure rating the pound to be now worth 5s 3d. Using this as a financial basis, and keeping an

eye on the fluctuations of purchase tax, a reasonable assessment is possible. The devaluation figures based on a pound in 1932 are these:

1932	..	.. £1	1958	..	.. 6s 6d
1935	..	.. 19s 2d	1960	..	.. 6s 4d
1938	..	.. 18s 5d	1961	..	.. 6s 2d
1942	..	.. 11s 0d	1962	..	.. 5s 11d
1946	..	.. 10s 9d	1963	..	.. 5s 9d
1949	..	.. 9s 1d	1964	..	.. 5s 7d
1952	..	.. 7s 8d	1965	..	.. 5s 4d
1955	..	.. 7s 3d	1966	..	.. 5s 3d

Calculations are made as follows:

Comparative present day value =

original cost × the devaluation figure for the year

5/3 (63 pence) being the present day value of the 1932 £1.

While the M-Type Midget, with its little 847 c.c. motor and all of its 20 b.h.p., has nothing in common with the current Mk. II other than its badge and the two webbing straps that retain the folded hood, no one will deny that for 1929, and for the gay young men for whom it was built, it was superb.

Having a top speed of 62 m.p.h. and a 0-60 time of 45 sec it would today be rated as expensive because at £185 then, it cost the equivalent of £705 now. But this car was a pioneer; this was the first time a small car with an interesting performance was available at anywhere near this price, and it appealed to a com-

M.G. TA (1936-39)

M.G. TC (1946-49)

Swept wing M.G. J2 (1932-34)

M.G. PB (1935-36)

pletely new section of our community.

Initially the M-Type appeared with a fabric-covered wooden body, but later with a more conventional metal one. The single overhead cam, 4-cylinder motor, even with its 2-bearing crank, was docile enough all through the rev. range, but nevertheless was noticeably happier towards the top end. Brakes have improved to such an extent since the M-Type was produced that an accurate assessment is difficult. However, fair comment can be made that in today's traffic an M-Type with the original cable brakes is somewhat of a liability unless considerable clearance is allowed at the higher speeds.

The M-Type was only the start, and after three years came the J-Type. Available at first with the cycle-type wings, and later in a swept-wing version, this model appealed as being a little more stylish. The engine was almost identical with the M's but the compression ratio had been raised from 5·4 to 6·2. The fuel tank was strapped on behind, giving what became a traditional profile, and the "noddy" appearance of the M-Type had disappeared. The J2 was 21 per cent quicker than the M. It had a top speed of 75 m.p.h., and could achieve a standing quarter-mile in 29·3 seconds. The sales were 2,300 in excess of the M,

and it was with the popular J2 that the enthusiast realized that he could push a Midget quite a long way past the makers' recommendations and get away with it—hence the J2 earned the reputation of having a rubber crankshaft.

It was indeed amazing what J2 cranks withstood, and while they did break from time to time, the problem could not be considered serious until most of the cranks in service had done considerable mileage with journals reground to well below the specifications. This was a credit to the original design, but if progress was to be maintained then something had to be done.

In 1934 the P-Type Midget appeared with a 3-bearing crank, other specifications being the same as the J2. Although top speed differed little from the J2, six seconds had been cut from the standing quarter, representing an improvement of 27·5 per cent in acceleration. The P-Type's 0-60 time of 23 sec was a 95 per cent improvement over the M of only two years earlier. The question of brakes had not been overlooked and the area was increased by fitting 12in. drums as standard, previously available only as an extra.

Road tests of the time report very favourably on the P-Type's improved suspension and roadholding, which for

pre-war standards was extremely good. The phase of P-Type production was concluded by the introduction of the PB with an extra 92 c.c., which gave an increase of 7 to 8 b.h.p. over the PA.

✻ In 1949 there was another change and the TD came out in almost complete sympathy with the Wolseley 4/44. The engine was the same XPAG unit as was fitted to the Wolseley and the TC, still developing 54·4 b.h.p. at 5,200 r.p.m. The main difference was that independent front suspension was fitted to the TD. The hard ride of 20 years' standing had disappeared. The front suspension assembly was very similar to that fitted to the Wolseley. The wheel size was reduced from 19in. to 15in., but the long, square radiator survived the onslaught of progress, and the TD made a very great impression on the market both at home and abroad. The former, however, must have been jeopardized by the crippling purchase tax. Indeed, both the TC and the TD were pioneers of sports car exports from this country to America and their contribution to British prestige cannot be over-rated.

While there was a very considerable improvement in road-holding and suspension, the TD was quite a bit heavier than the TC, yet with the same engine this resulted in very little difference in

✻Continued on page 43

M.G. TD (1950-53)

M.G. TF (1954-55)

AUTOCAR, 13 May 1966

M.G. Midget Mk I (1961-1963)   M.G. Midget Mk II (1964 onwards)

M.G. Midget Analysis . . .

their comparative performances. Road tests, reports and experience do not consistently place either as being the faster—on acceleration or top speed. A slightly faster version—the TD II, developing 57 b.h.p. at 5,500 r.p.m.—was available from 1950 onwards.

During TD production between 1950 and 1953 purchase tax played havoc with value-for-money on the retail price. A TD with a basic price of £530 was loaded with £222 purchase tax. The comparative figure today for the basic price is £775, so again the manufacturers had made their contribution by changing from the TC to the TD for an increase which has a current equivalent of only £62, and was indeed worth every penny. Again this was denied to the British public who had to pay £752 for a TD which has a current equivalent of £1,095, so the value-to-cost ratio had been destroyed.

Good-looker

Worse, however, was still to come. The TF which replaced the TD in 1954 is considered by many to be the best-looking car that has ever come from Abingdon. The bonnet had been lowered, the headlamps incorporated in the wings, and the traditional flat facia panel had disappeared. Fitted with the optional wire wheels this was unquestionably a very inspiring machine. It performed on a parallel with the TD II, having the same engine and compression ratio of 8·1 to 1. This TF retailed at £780. The retailing therefore cost the public £28 over the price of the TD. The change for this price was an exceptional return for the extra money.

The Government, however, did not relent. Tax on the TF was in the region of £230 and, together with the basic price it retailed at £780 which has a current equivalent of £1,114. While the TF was a classic and quality car, and its suspension, road-holding and brakes were impeccable this was too much to pay for a Midget that was only marginally quicker than the 1939 TB.

In the following year, 1955, a new TF was available with the engine capacity increased to 1,500 c.c. developing 63 b.h.p. at 5,500 r.p.m. This gave the substantial increase in performance of about 7 per cent over the 1,250 TF and the TD II. The revised 1,500 engine, designated XPEG, was perhaps a little less robust than its predecessor, the XPAG.

Tradition Ends

The TF was the last of the traditionally styled Midgets, and there was another outcry when its production ceased. The subsequent model was the MGA, a new style incorporating the 1,500 B-series motor, and rightly it was decided that this could hardly be called a Midget. The Midget then disappeared for six years. The devaluation of the 1932 £1 during that time was 1s 1d. By an amalgamation of development costs with Austin-Healey, and a wider spread of overheads through increased production the next Midget appeared in 1961 at a very competitive price.

The 1961 Midget was a small, compact, unit-construction sports car. Its 948 c.c. motor developed just over 46 b.h.p. at 5,500 r.p.m. Its time for the standing quarter was comparable with the TC's, but its 0-60 time was almost 3 sec quicker. The basic price was £472 but purchase tax was still crippling at £217. It is interesting to compare the current equivalent of the basic price which is £554 with the corresponding figure for the M-Type, or indeed any

of the previous Midgets. This was by far the lowest price for which a Midget until then had been produced. It could offer everything except the classical configuration of its predecessors but unfortunately retailed at a comparative figure of £809. The 948 c.c. Midget was followed by an almost identical car with a 1,098 c.c. motor, and incorporating disc brakes on the front wheels. This car was 3·1 sec quicker over the standing quarter and 1·9 sec quicker on the 0-60 time.

It was now that the impediment of purchase tax was to be somewhat lightened. The 1,098 Mk. I, as it is known, cost basically £478 plus £120 purchase tax which gave a retail price of £599. This has a current equivalent of £675, and this, therefore, is the first Midget to be offered to the public for less than the M-Type of 1932. There is no need to stress the differences, or what may be termed progress. The value for money speaks for itself.

In 1964 the 1,098 Mk. II Midget came out with a curved windscreen, wind-up side window, half elliptic rear-springs and a more robust crank. This one is 2·5 sec quicker than the 1,098 Mk. I on a 0-60 time, and 0·8 seconds quicker over the standing quarter. There was a 4 per cent improvement in top speed, which according to road tests now stands at 92 m.p.h.

The Mk. II Midget is an exceptionally fine car, and at £624 is sold at the lowest comparative price at which a Midget has ever been put on the market in this country. It must represent the finest value for money that has ever come from Abingdon. Its exceptional qualities put the Mk. II in a class on its own. There are fewer than a handful of production sports cars that are anywhere near a match for a properly driven Mk. II Midget across its homeland of rural England.   **Peter Poyntz-Wright** ∎

M.G. Midget Mk. II with an Ashley fast-back hard-top

Year	Model	Basic price	Tax	Retail price	Relative value of 1932 £1	Relative value of basic	Relative value of retail	b.h.p.	Standing ½-sec	0-60 sec
1929–32 ..	M	£185	—	£185	20s	£705	£705	20	—	45·0
1932–34 ..	J1 and J2	£200	—	£200	20s	£762	£762	36	29·3	—
1934–35 ..	P	£222	—	£222	19s 2d	£810	£810	35*	23·0	23·0
1936–39 ..	TA	£222	—	£222	18s 5d	£778	£778	50	22·8	—
1946–49 ..	TC	£412	£115	£527	10s 9d	£845	£1,079	54·4	21·8	21·1
	TC	£412	£115	£527	9s 1d	£713	£912	54·4	21·8	21·1
1950–53 ..	TD	£530	£222	£752	7s 8d	£775	£1,095	54·4†	23·2	23·6
1954 ..	TF	£550	£230	£780	7s 6d	£787	£1,114	57·3	23·0	23·3
1955 ..	TF	£645	£270	£915	7s 3d	£898	£1,264	63	—	—
1961 ..	948	£472	£217	£689	6s 2d	£554	£809	46	21·6	18·3
1962 ..	1098 I	£478	£120	£599	5s 11d	£540	£675	55	20·5	16·4
1964 ..	1098 II	£512	£111	£623	5s 7d	£546	£663	59	19·7	13·9
1966 ..	1098 II	£512	£111	£623	5s 3d	£512	£623	59	19·7	13·9

*PB 43 b.h.p. 1935–36. †TD II 57 b.h.p.

❋Continued from page 41

MIDGETS ANALYSIS

IN the article " A Comparative Analysis of Midgets—1929 to 1965," published in last week's issue of Autocar, a substantial part of Peter Poyntz-Wright's story was inadvertently omitted by the printers. We apologize to readers, who must have wondered, for example, what had happened to the famous M.G. TC, of which no mention was made other than in the captions to photographs. The " lost " galley of type follows, and should be read between the first and second paragraphs in column three of page 975, running on from " . . . an increase of 7 to 8 b.h.p. over the PA."

THE superior qualities of the P-Types, especially acceleration, were a first-class return for an increase of only 11 per cent in the retail price over the J2. Purchase tax played no part in these early years, and the P-Type price of £222, giving a current equivalent of £810, for pre-war development years, must be considered extremely reasonable.

The P-Type was the last of the overhead-cam Midgets. It *did* mark the end of an era, and there was the first of what has become a fairly regular howl of protest at any serious and progressive change made at Abingdon.

Nevertheless it was essential to keep the Midget on a parallel with standard bread and butter line. The 10 h.p. Morris-Wolseley push-rod unit was the one selected for the next Midget—the TA. A wet clutch and the innovation of synchromesh gave the sceptics ammunition, but the whole assembly performed extremely well. There was a substantial increase of 353 c.c. over the P-Types at 1,292 c.c., but it is doubtful if the increase in performance could have been achieved with a comparatively slow revving push-rod engine of this type without it.

The TA came out at the same price as the PB in 1936, retailing at £222. In terms of comparative performance it was an improvement over the P-Type. Having a 0-50 time of 15·2 sec it was

12½ per cent quicker than the PA on initial acceleration, and there was a 5 per cent improvement on top speed.

A push-rod engine in a sports car in 1936 was something of a novelty. However, it was certainly the right answer—it produced 50 b.h.p. at the comparatively low engine speed of 4,000 r.p.m., compared with the PB's 43 at a considerably higher engine speed. The extra power called for the substantial improvement in braking that was supplied by fitting hydraulically operated 9in. drums. This was the first time hydraulic brakes had been fitted as standard equipment to a Midget.

The TA was longer and lower-slung than any that had gone before, and heralded the classic lines of the post-war TC. The TA appealed to a slightly wider range of followers than the earlier designs, which were more often used for competition than fast touring.

The amazing thing is that taking comparative values the TA cost £778, which was £32 less than its immediate predecessor, the PB, and it had improved lines, power and brakes. It was only 11 per cent up on the comparative price of the M-Type of seven years earlier, over which it was 29 per cent faster on top speed.

The TA continued until May 1939, by which time some 3,000 had been built. Then followed the TB, using a slightly smaller motor of 1,250 c.c. with a dry clutch and a new gearbox that was acclaimed as being " of a new standard of mechanical perfection." The engine was a slightly faster revving unit than the TA's, and was the first with shell bearings to be fitted to a Midget. It supplied an increase in power of 4·4 b.h.p. In external appearances the TA and TB were almost identical, with a few small details that could be used for identification, but even these were inconsistent. The TB was in fact 4in. wider than the TA, but this was not immediately apparent to the observer. Unfortunately, the TB was destined for a very brief production period, and by

the outbreak of war only 380 had been made.

After the war the TB was not continued, but with a few small modifications reappeared as the most famous Midget of all—the TC, a truly remarkable car that caught the imagination of thousands all over the world. It was 10 per cent quicker than the TA in achieving a 0-50 time of 13·9 sec. The springing was hard but for the first time piston-type dampers were used. The sliding trunnions in use since 1932 now gave way to shackles

At the arrival of the TC in 1945, the 1932 £1 was worth only 10s 9d, and the arch enemy of enterprise had darkened our doors—purchase tax had arrived. The manufacturers had done their share by having a prestige sports car, of exceptional performance for 1946, in series-production at a basic cost, in comparative figures, of £845. This would have been exceptional value, and the increase in price of only 9 per cent over the TA, incorporating a six-year production stoppage, is remarkable and can be attributed only to astute businessmen who were devoted enthusiasts. Unfortunately their achievement was denied to the British public who were required to pay £115 (now £234) purchase tax, which raised the comparative price to £1,079. Progress had definitely been achieved. The TC could cover a standing quarter in 21·8 sec, an increase of 34 per cent over the J2, and its 0-60 time of 21·1 is a 216 per cent improvement on the 45 sec of the M-Type.

Between 1946 and 1949 devaluation had caused a drop in value of 1s 8d in the £1 of 1932. The TC, therefore, in its later years was available at current comparative prices of down to £912, which included purchase tax. Production of the TC continued unchanged for four years. It was the last and finest of the spoked-wheel, cart-sprung Midgets, and for the more romantic enthusiast will always retain a certain magic charm, especially for those privileged in having, at sometime, owned one. ∎

MG — CLIMAX

(Continued from page 13)

impaired by the much-increased power output.

Roadholding, in fact, is extremely good on smooth surfaces, and handling is almost up to sports/racing standards — thanks to the Midget's very precise steering and an anti-roll bar which virtually eliminates this model's characteristic roll oversteer.

On bumpy corners, however, the

car tends to hop about somewhat and the ride is generally rather firm —as on all Midgets and Sprites. Brabham now plans to soften the rear springs — to improve both road-holding and ride — and also fit a Panhard rod.

Besides the disc brakes and an anti-roll bar, I would recommend fitting a hardtop as another essential adjunct for fast motoring. The standard soft top is extremely noisy at anything over 80 m.p.h. It also tends to lift away from the top of the windscreen at higher-than-standard speeds, but is prevented from blowing off by

fasteners at each end of the screen. The exhaust note also becomes rather obtrusive at over 5000 r.p.m., although the Midget muffler is very effective at lower engine speeds.

Externally, the Midget-Climax is indistinguishable from a standard model. This feature, in conjunction with its ability to out-accelerate all mass-produced sports cars under 3 litres, will give it a special appeal for many people. And for anyone who wants a fast, small sports car with character, Jack's latest creation could well be the answer. ●●●

MG Midget

GREAT BRITAIN

ENGINE CAPACITY 77.80 cu in, 1,275 cu cm
FUEL CONSUMPTION 31.4 m/imp gal, 26.1 m/US gal, 9 l × 100 km
SEATS 2 **MAX SPEED** 92 mph, 148 km/h
PRICE IN GB basic £ 555, total £ 684

ENGINE front, 4 stroke; cylinders: 4, vertical, in line; bore and stroke: 2.78 × 3.20 in, 70.6 × 81.3 mm; engine capacity: 77.80 cu in, 1,275 cu cm; compression ratio: 8.8; max power (DIN): 65 hp at 6,000 rpm; max torque (DIN): 65 lb ft, 9 kg m at 3,000 rpm; max engine rpm: 6,000; specific power: 51 hp/l; cylinder block: cast iron; cylinder head: cast iron; crankshaft bearings: 3; valves: 2 per cylinder, overhead, push-rods and rockers; camshafts: 1, side; lubrication: eccentric pump, full flow filter; lubricating system capacity: 7 imp pt, 8.46 US pt, 7 l; carburation: 2 SU type HS 2 semi-downdraught carburettors; fuel feed: electric pump; cooling system: water; cooling system capacity: 10.50 imp pt, 12.68 US pt, 6 l.

TRANSMISSION driving wheels: rear; clutch: single dry plate, hydraulically controlled; gearbox: mechanical; gears: 4 + reverse; synchromesh gears: II, III, IV; gearbox ratios: I 3.200, II 1.916, III 1.357, IV 1, rev 4.114; gear lever: central; final drive: hypoid bevel; axle ratio: 4.220.

CHASSIS integral; front suspension: independent, wishbones, coil springs, lever dampers as upper arms; rear suspension: rigid axle, semi-elliptic leafsprings, lever dampers.

STEERING rack-and-pinion; turns of steering wheel lock to lock: 2.30.

BRAKES front disc (diameter 8 in, 203 mm), rear drum; area rubbed by linings: front 135 sq in, 870.75 sq cm, rear 55 sq in, 354.75 sq cm, total 190 sq in, 1,225.50 sq cm.

ELECTRICAL EQUIPMENT voltage: 12 V; battery: 43 Ah; generator type: dynamo, 22 Ah; ignition distributor: Lucas; headlamps: 2.

DIMENSIONS AND WEIGHT wheel base: 80 in, 2,032 mm; front track: 46.31 in, 1,176 mm; rear track: 44.75 in, 1,137 mm; overall length: 137.62 in, 3,495 mm; overall width: 54.87 in, 1,394 mm; overall height: 49.75 in, 1,264 mm; ground clearance: 5 in, 127 mm; dry weight: 1,510 lb, 685 kg; distribution of weight: 52.4% front axle, 47.6% rear axle; turning circle (between walls): 32 ft, 9.8 m; tyres: 5.20 × 13; fuel tank capacity: 6 imp gal, 7.1 US gal, 27 l.

BODY convertible; doors: 2; seats: 2.

PERFORMANCE max speeds: 29 mph, 46.7 km/h in 1st gear; 49 mph, 78.9 km/h in 2nd gear; 69 mph, 111 km/h in 3rd gear; 92 mph, 148 km/h in 4th gear; power-weight ratio: 23.2 lb/hp, 10.5 kg/hp; carrying capacity: 353 lb, 160 kg; acceleration: standing ¼ mile 20.1 sec, 0 — 50 mph (0 — 80 km/h) 9.9 sec; speed in direct drive at 1,000 rpm: 15.5 mph, 25 km/h.

PRACTICAL INSTRUCTIONS fuel: 98 oct petrol; engine sump oil: 6.40 imp pt, 7.61 US pt, 3.6 l, SAE 20W-30 (winter) 20W-40 (summer), change every 6,000 miles, 9,700 km; gearbox oil: 2.25 imp pt, 2.75 US pt, 1.3 l, SAE 10W-30 (winter) 20W-40 (summer), change every 6,000 miles, 9,700 km; final drive oil: 1.50 imp pt, 1.69 US pt, 0.8 l, SAE 90; greasing: every 3,000 miles, 4,800 km, 10 points; tappet clearances: inlet 0.012 in, 0.30 mm, exhaust 0.012 in, 0.30 mm; normal tyre pressure: front 18 psi, 1.3 atm, rear 20 psi, 1.4 atm.

VARIATIONS AND OPTIONAL ACCESSORIES oil cooler; wire wheels and knock-on hubs; anti-roll bar on front suspension; hardtop.

Autocar
ROAD
TEST
NUMBER 2118

HOF 867D

M.G. Midget III 1,275 c.c.

AT A GLANCE: Latest version of popular small M.G.—Austin-Healey range. Slightly better acceleration and mid-range torque than previous model. Robust engine and transmission, with full range of B.M.C. tuning equipment available. Excellent gearchange but no synchromesh on bottom gear. M.p.g. little affected by more powerful engine. Sports car ride and handling in best M.G. traditions. Faultless brakes. New hood a great improvement, but cramped seating not changed. Inadequate heater control.

MANUFACTURER
The M.G. Car Co. Ltd., Abingdon-on-Thames, Berkshire.

PRICES

Basic	..	..	..	£555	0s 0d
Purchase Tax	..		..	£128	18s 2d
Total (in G.B.)		..	..	£683	18s 2d

EXTRAS (inc. P.T.)

Wire wheels (factory fitted)		£30	14s 7d
Heater	..	£14	15s 0d

PERFORMANCE SUMMARY

Mean maximum speed	93·5 m.p.h.
Standing start ¼-mile..	19·7 sec
0-60 m.p.h.	14·6 sec
30-70 m.p.h. (through gears)	16·1 sec
Fuel consumption ..	30 m.p.g.
Miles per tankful ..	180

EIGHT-AND-A-HALF years of consistent development by the B.M.C. sports car factory at Abingdon have improved the Sprite-Midget range in nearly every respect. Few Mark I Sprite owners would argue that their version is still the best, and they would be hard put to recognize many parts of the latest car. Our test car on this occasion was the M.G. Midget Series III which, apart from the badges and some trim details, is identical with the Series IV Austin-Healey Sprite. In fact the first M.G. Midget appeared as a more luxurious version of the new Series II Sprite in June 1961, and the latest 1,275 c.c. engined car is really the fourth distinct development.

The original Midget had the 948 c.c. engine, a much simpler facia design, styling almost identical with the latest car, sliding windows and a " build-it-yourself " hood. Later this model was given the new 1,098 c.c. engine and disc brakes became standard. In March 1964 the Mk. II model appeared, fitted for the first time with wind-up windows and half-elliptic rear springs, plus revised interior trim. Finally the latest Mark III version was released just in time for the last Earls Court show. Production cars are only now appearing

on British roads, as there have been some delays in building up output and the vast majority of Midgets are destined for valuable export markets.

Though the latest car has a 1,275 c.c. engine, superficially the same as that of the famous 1275S Mini-Cooper, it has been detuned somewhat to keep down the cost. In place of the Cooper S's nitrided-steel crankshaft there is a normal forged one, and the Mark II Midget camshaft timing replaces that of the S. Compression ratio is down a little, valves and ports a little restricted, and both inlet and exhaust manifolds are the same as on previous Midgets. There has been no change to gearbox or rear axle, though a diaphragm spring clutch is now fitted. Claimed power output is 65 b.h.p. at 6,000 r.p.m. instead of the 59 b.h.p. at 5,750 r.p.m. of the previous model.

Because the new car has 6 b.h.p. more than the 1,100 c.c. which it replaces, and because there has been a negligible weight increase with no change to the gearing, we were expecting to find significant performance gains. Mysteriously, the 1,275 c.c. car was only just as lively as the 1,100 we last sampled in April 1964. This car, in its turn, was *much* livelier than a previous 1,100 test car with 3 b.h.p. less (56 b.h.p.). We can

▶

Autocar Road Test number 2118

Make: M.G.

Type: MIDGET III 1,275 c.c.

TEST CONDITIONS
Weather: Frosty and clear. Wind 5–10 m.p.h.
Temperature: 2 deg. C. (36 deg. F.)
Barometer: 29·6 in. Hg.
Surfaces: Dry concrete and asphalt

Figures taken at 5,400 miles by our own staff at the Motor Industry Research Association proving ground at Nuneaton.

WEIGHT
Kerb weight: 14·2cwt (1,589lb-721kg) (with oil, water and half-full fuel tank)
Distribution, per cent F, 52; R, 48.
Laden as tested: 17·9cwt (2,011lb-912kg)

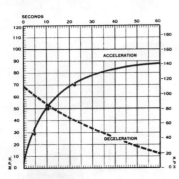

MAXIMUM SPEEDS

Gear	m.p.h.	k.p.h.	r.p.m.
Top (mean)	93·5	150	6,070
(best)	95	153	6,170
3rd	71	114	6,300
2nd	50	81	6,300
1st	30	48	6,300

Standing ¼-Mile 19·7 sec 68 m.p.h.
Standing Kilometre 37·4 sec 82 m.p.h.

TIME IN SECONDS	4·6	7·0	9·9	14·6	20·7	33·2	
TRUE SPEED M.P.H.	30	40	50	60	70	80	90
INDICATED SPEED	31	42	52	62	72	83	93

Mileage recorder 1 per cent over-reading. Test distance 1,179 miles.

Speed range, gear ratios and time in seconds

m.p.h.	Top (4·22)	3rd (5·73)	2nd (8·09)	1st (13·50)
10—30	—	7·7	4·7	3·3
20—40	10·6	7·5	4·4	—
30—50	9·8	6·5	5·4	—
40—60	10·0	8·0	—	—
50—70	12·4	10·2	—	—
60—80	17·1	—	—	—

FUEL CONSUMPTION

(At constant speeds—m.p.g.)

30 m.p.h.	40·0
40	41·2
50	40·0
60	35·4
70	31·7
80	28·5

Typical m.p.g. 30 (9·4 litres/100 km)
Calculated (DIN) m.p.g. 28·8 (9·8 litres/100km)

Overall m.p.g. 28·4 (9·95 litres/100km)

Grade of fuel, Premium (96·8-98·8 RM)

OIL CONSUMPTION
Miles per pint (SAE 10W/30)   800

BRAKES (from 30 m.p.h. in neutral)

Load	g	Distance
25 lb	0·19	158ft
50 ,,	0·44	68 ,,
75 ,,	0·70	43 ,,
100 ,,	1·00	30·1 ,,
Handbrake	0·42	72 ,,

Max. Gradient, 1 in 3
Clutch Pedal: 35 lb and 4in.

TURNING CIRCLES
Between kerbs L, 32ft 0in.; R, 31ft 3in.
Between walls L, 33ft 3in.; R, 32ft 6in.
Steering wheel turns, lock to lock, 2·3.

HOW THE CAR COMPARES:

MAXIMUM SPEED (mean) M.P.H.
M.G. Midget III
B.M.C. 1275S Mini-Cooper
Fiat 850 Coupe
Sunbeam Imp Sport
Triumph Spitfire II

0-60 M.P.H. (secs)
M.G. Midget III
B.M.C. 1275S Mini-Cooper
Fiat 850 Coupe
Sunbeam Imp Sport
Triumph Spitfire II

STANDING START ¼ MILE (secs)
M.G. Midget III
B.M.C. 1275S Mini-Cooper
Fiat 850 Coupe
Sunbeam Imp Sport
Triumph Spitfire II

M.P.G. OVERALL
M.G. Midget III
B.M.C. 1275S Mini-Cooper
Fiat 850 Coupe
Sunbeam Imp Sport
Triumph Spitfire II

PRICES

M.G. Midget III	£684
Mini-Cooper 1275S	£849
Fiat 850 Coupé	£865
Sunbeam Imp Sport	£665
Triumph Spitfire II	£678

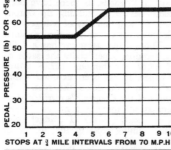

The M.G. Midget's Mk I Sprite ancestry is still evident below waist level. The chromium strip which permanently attaches the back of the hood to the body is the only outward feature identifying the Mk III from its predecessor

M.G. MIDGET III

only assume now that the 1964 test car was perhaps in better-than-average form at the time, while the subject of this test is a thoroughly representative 1,275 c.c. Midget. Comparison of its performance with other sports cars having similar power-weight ratios confirms this, and two owners of late model 1,100s reckoned that there were, indeed, substantial gains with the new car.

With its bigger, though less highly tuned engine, the new Midget is more docile than before, needing little cosseting to develop its full performance on the open road. The torque delivery is smooth throughout the range, and no Midget owner should be frightened away from town traffic jams by thoughts of temperament. In top gear the little car can be trundled along at a mere 800 r.p.m. (12 m.p.h.) and can be accelerated smoothly, without snatch or hesitation from 10 m.p.h. if necessary. Acceleration figures for this range were not taken, as the practice is not likely to be used on such a sporting car.

By the time 2,000 r.p.m. is reached, everything is beginning to swing together, though most owners will be stirring the gear lever about to make sure the needle is always above 4,000 r.p.m. It is all too easy to over-rev, unless a careful watch is kept on the rev-counter, and there is little doubt that well over 6,500 r.p.m. could be seen in the indirect gears. In deference to the danger markings on the rev-counter we changed gear at 6,300 r.p.m. when conducting performance tests; the engine was then well on to the meat of the power curve at the same road speed in the next gear. The fastest standing starts were achieved by using 4,500 r.p.m. and controlled clutch slip off the line.

Full choke is needed for rapid cold-starts, though the engine warms up quickly, and the choke knob can be pushed home after the first half mile or so. When thoroughly warm, helped by the perfectly balanced S.U. carburettors on this test car, the idling speed is a gentle 700 r.p.m.

At higher speeds, however, mechanical noise increased quite considerably. At 70 m.p.h. the engine is turning at 4,550 r.p.m. and this, together with the usual wind noise around the hood, made normal conversation difficult. Reception from the optional Radiomobile was excellent, but difficult to enjoy because of the high noise level. There appears to be no sound-deadening material between the engine bay and the cockpit. Despite the low overall gearing, and the spirited way in which we usually drove the car, its oil pressure never fluctuated; most of the time this stabilized at between 70 and 80 p.s.i. If anything, the car is a little overcooled, for we never managed to get the water temperature above about 162 deg. F. (72 deg. C.), which is just about the thermostat-opening point.
▶

The very functional cockpit has its tachometer and speedometer angled towards the driver's line of vision. The driver can erect the hood without getting out of the car

Left: Accessibility to the oil filter, distributor and battery is not easy. The handwheel in front of the heater assembly controls the heater temperature. Right: Boot space is limited by the spare wheel and hood cover. The stay is held by the clip at the corner of the boot lid

M.G. MIDGET III

One of the delights of every Austin-Healey Sprite and M.G. Midget has been the splendid gearbox and gearchange. With the gear lever knob only inches from the steering wheel rim, it really does "fall readily to hand"; gearchange movements are short, ultra-light and just as fast as required. Though the baulk-ring synchromesh is efficient on top, 3rd and 2nd, the Midget is one of the few British cars which has an unsynchronized bottom gear. At low speeds in traffic the driver often feels the need to thrust down into bottom gear for a speedy take-off, but we found more than usually accurate double-declutching was needed to make a silent change. All the indirect gears, particularly bottom (with straight-cut teeth) are noisy, and somewhat harsh.

Perhaps, too, the ratios are a little widely spaced, yet somehow the Midget's change typifies everything that is enjoyable in sports car driving, and an owner will find himself "stirring up the cogs" just for the fun of it. The latest clutch is a diaphragm spring type. Though smaller than before, its operation was smooth, and no amount of abuse caused any judder or slipping.

No red-blooded young owner (or *Autocar* tester, for that matter) would think of driving such a lively little sports car slowly, and the overall fuel consumption must have suffered a little because of the use we gave it. During 1,200 miles of exuberant motoring we averaged 28.4 m.p.g.; this compares very well with 29.7 m.p.g. for the 1964 1,100, and 29.1 for an earlier (1963) 1,100 Sprite. Steady speed fuel consumption measurements above 50 m.p.h. were very similar to the earlier model, but at lower (traffic) speeds, the new car was much thirstier. As compression ratio is only 8.8 to 1, normal premium fuel is perfectly adequate.

As with all previous Sprites and

Midgets, the 6-gallon fuel tank is really much too small. On our test car a gauge fault meant that barely 110 miles (and about 4 gallons) were completed before the unsteady needle began to indicate "Empty." A normal fuel range, without taking risks, would be 150 miles; though barely adequate by day, a long night journey might present problems when filling stations are few and far between.

Big improvements were made to the Midget's rear suspension when the Mark II was introduced in 1964; the original cantilever quarter-elliptics were replaced by conventional half-elliptic leaf springs. Since then there have been no important changes, and the Mark III Midget handles just like the previous model. Following the very best M.G. roadholding traditions, the ride is firm, perhaps even a little choppy on minor roads, while the steering is light, positive and direct. Urging the little car down simulated "rally roads" seemed to need only tiny wrist movements on the wheel, and the Midget must be one of very few cars which seems to go exactly where it is pointed. With very little understeer to make rapid direction changes untidy, the little car's handling is delicately balanced and enjoyable. When pressed really hard, the tail begins to break away apologetically; this can be curbed by the merest flick of opposite lock, almost without thinking. In fact, the Midget must be one of the safest cars on the road when in the right hands. Roll is strictly limited at all times, and damping firm.

Predictably, the little car does not enjoy being forced down rough roads, which can provoke some occasional axle tramp. The structure felt impressively rigid at all times.

Fade-free braking and a predictable pedal response is now expected from modern disc-drum systems; the Lockheed layout fitted to this Midget was no exception. In normally hard road use, there was no increase in pedal travel, and even the rigorous fade tests carried out at MIRA did not show up any limitations. The hand-

brake (surprisingly not with a fly-off release) was efficient, allowing 42 per cent braking when used alone, and holding the car easily on a 1-in-3 test gradient.

The latest Midget's driving position is disappointing and somewhat cramped. Late model Mark II Midgets were given revised seats, similar to those of the MGB, which are retained on the new model. Their back rests are thicker than before, with less bucket shaping, though they hold passengers in place quite well against high cornering forces. Unfortunately the thicker back rests have restricted the small living space still more, and drivers taller than 5ft 8in. found it difficult to get comfortable. Rearward seat adjustment is limited by a structural bulkhead behind the slides, while the steering wheel and facia panel are uncompromisingly near to the driver's shoulders. The now customary straight-arm driving position is quite impossible in the Midget, and long-legged drivers found their legs wrapped unhappily around the steering column. Heel-and-toe gear changing is possible without effort, but there is no real resting place for an unoccupied clutch foot.

To be really in fashion, modern sports car must have a foldaway hood; that fitted to the new Midget is much better than the previous type and certainly the most worthwhile improvement in the new car. Two stout overcentre catches and a couple of press studs attach the hood to the screen rail. Furling the hood to its stowed position can be done in one sweep from inside the car. The press-studs near to the door hinges should be released, or the hood fabric might be torn in folding down. When erect, windproofing is excellent, and during our fortnight's test there were no water leaks. Though the new hood has a lower profile than before, there seemed to be ample headroom for tall passengers. When furled, part of the useful stowage space behind the seats is obstructed; there is a neat hood cover.

The Midget's heater is still a £15

AUTOCAR, 9 February 1967

extra though it woud be difficult to order a car for home delivery without one. Its control and adjustment is crude and unsatisfactory for many conditions. A water tap under the bonnet controls supply of warm water to the matrix, while the only air or temperature control in the car is by opening or closing flaps in the foot-wells. A switch on the facia operates the booster fan. There are no fresh air vents.

For such a small car the luggage boot seems quite large, though the floor is practically filled by the spare wheel, jack and tools, and the surfaces are unlined. The boot lid, like the bonnet, has to be propped open by a stay. On our test car the boot-lid stay was already damaging paintwork near its clip.

The small-sized popular-price sports car market is expanding all the time, and buyers continue to demand improvements in performance and specification. By regular power in-creases and trim changes B.M.C. have kept abreast of the trends; un-doubtedly the M.G. Midget will be with us for some time yet. ∎

SPECIFICATION: M.G. MIDGET III (FRONT ENGINE, REAR-WHEEL DRIVE)

ENGINE
Cylinders	..	4, in line
Cooling system	..	Water; pump, fan and ther-mostat
Bore	..	70·6mm (2·78in.)
Stroke	..	81·3mm (3·2in.)
Displacement	..	1,275 c.c. (78 cu. in.)
Valve gear	..	Overhead, push rods and rockers
Compression ratio	8·8-to-1	
Carburettors	..	2 S.U. H.S.2
Fuel pump	..	S.U. Electric
Oil filter	..	Full flow with renewable element
Max. power	..	65 b.h.p. (net) at 6,000 r.p.m.
Max. torque	..	72 lb. ft. (net) at 3,000 r.p.m.

TRANSMISSION
Clutch	..	Borg and Beck diaphragm spring 6·5in. dia.
Gearbox	..	4-speed, synchromesh on Top, 3rd and 2nd
Gear ratios	..	Top 1·00; Third 1·36; Second 1·92; First 3·20; Reverse 4·11
Final drive	..	Hypoid bevel, 4·22 to 1

CHASSIS and BODY
Construction	..	Integral, with steel body, fold away hood

SUSPENSION
Front	..	Independent, coil springs, wishbones, lever-arm dampers
Rear	..	Live axle, half-elliptic leaf springs, lever-arm dampers

STEERING
Type	..	Cam Gears, rack and pinion
Wheel dia.		15·5in.

BRAKES
Make and type	..	Lockheed disc front, drum rear
Servo	..	None
Dimensions	..	F, 8·25in. dia. R, 7.0in. dia. 1·25in. wide shoes
Swept area	..	F, 135 sq. in.; R, 55 sq. in. Total 190 sq. in. (237 sq.in.) per ton laden

WHEELS
Type	..	Wire-spoked centre lock (optional extra). 3·5in. wide rim
Tyres—make	..	Dunlop
—type		C41 Nylon tubed cross-ply
—size	..	5·20—13in.

EQUIPMENT
Battery	..	12-volt 43-amp. hr.
Generator	..	22 amp. d.c.
Headlamps	..	Lucas sealed beam 45/40-watt
Reversing lamp	..	None
Electric fuses	..	2
Screen wipers	..	Single speed, self parking
Screen washer	..	Standard, manual plunger
Interior heater	..	Extra, fresh air type
Safety belts	..	Extra, anchorages built in
Interior trim	..	Leather seats, PVC hood

Floor covering	..	Carpet
Starting handle		No provision
Jack	..	Screw pillar
Jacking points	..	One each side, under door
Windscreen	..	Zone toughened
Underbody pro-tection	..	Cellulose paint only
Other bodies	..	Hardtop

MAINTENANCE
Fuel tank	..	6 Imp. gallons (no reserve) (27 litres)
Cooling system	..	10·5 pints (including heater) (6 pints)
Engine sump	..	6·5 pints (3·7 litres) SAE 10W/30. Change oil and element every 6,000 miles
Gearbox	..	2·2 pints SAE 30. No change necessary after first 500 miles
Final drive	..	1·5 pints SAE 90. No change necessary after first 500 miles
Grease	..	10 points every 3,000 miles
Tyre pressures	..	F, 18; R, 20 p.s.i. (normal driving). F, 22; R, 24 p.s.i. (fast driving).

PERFORMANCE DATA
Top gear m.p.h. per 1,000 r.p.m.	15·4
Mean piston speed at max. power	3,200ft./min.
B.h.p. per ton laden	81·1

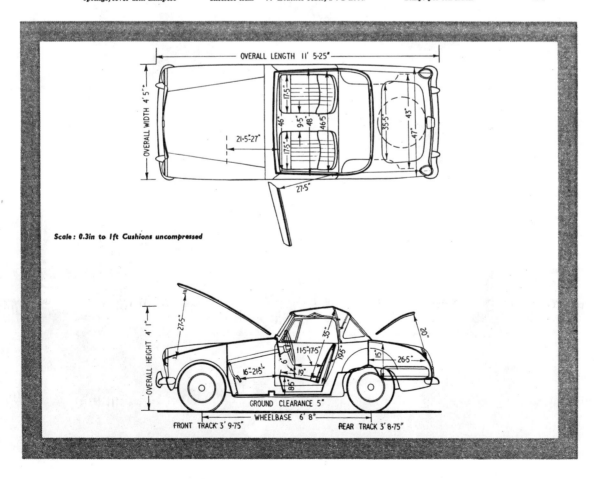

Scale: 0.3in to 1ft Cushions uncompressed

Road Test: MG Midget Mk.III
SAFETY FASTER, ALREADY

Two major changes denote the Mk. III Sprite and MG Midget: a 1275-cc engine and a fold-down top. The engine enhances the performance and the top completes the general convenience and weatherproofing that make it a more modern sports car. After that what do you say? Well, you look at the car and then the base price of $2095 for the Sprite and $2250 for the Midget (wire wheels and trim make the difference). Then you have to conclude that both are outstanding buys on the low end of the sports-car price scale.

The ride and handling remain pretty much unchanged; a bit choppy on the ride and relatively good in the corners. The power plant, developing 65 horsepower at 6000 rpm, features a nitrided crankshaft. It gets the little machine through the standing quarter-mile in 19.4 seconds and from 0-60 mph in 12.7 seconds. It may do even better with more break-in time than our test car had. Gas mileage averages about 28 miles per gallon for normal commuting and around-town running, quite a bit higher on the highway. Top speed is close to 90 mph, depending on which direction the wind is blowing.

Still unchanged, but a relatively minor annoyance is the non-synchro First in the quick-shifting four-speed gearbox. The brakes, with 8¼-inch discs front and seven-inch drums in the rear, are excellent. Body dimensions are the same; entry and exit are cramped but, once you're seated, there's ample room.

With more performance and the absence of the do-it-yourself convertible top, the car is an even more attractive buy for someone who wants a solid, fun-type tiddler that'll take them most anywhere for the lowest in both purchase *and* operating costs. We happened to have four different cars at home during the Midget's test period. Somehow, it was always the one we hopped in to go someplace. It got the job done the quickest and easiest.

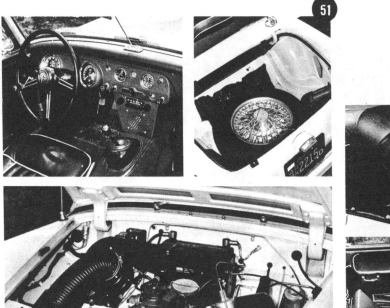

Featured: full instru-
mentation, almost
humorous lack of luggage
space, good upholstery
and finish, strong 1.3-liter
engine with expensive,
nitrided crankshaft, neat
fold-down top with
smoother line.

BMC buries the Austin Healey Sprite, but revives a famous name, the MG Midget

meet the midget

THERE'S a good deal of commonsense behind BMC's decision to drop the Austin Healey Sprite and replace it with the almost identical MG Midget.

Despite the fact that MGs aren't the force in competition that they used to be, the name still commands a lot of respect, and consequently draws customers like flies to a honey pot.

The Austin Healey name-tag, while appreciated by the hard core sports car initiates, didn't have the same appeal to run-of-the-mill customers.

The Sprite continues in production back in the Old Dart, but you won't be able to buy one here.

MG dealers have been importing Midgets independently of BMC for some time—since the Sprite went out of production, in fact—but local manufacture will begin at BMC's Zetland establishment soon.

We recently spent a few hours behind the wheel of the Midget, and we'll shortly be getting it for a full-length road test.

The motor is the B-series donk, producing 65 bhp from 1275 cc (bore 70.61 mm, stroke 81.28 mm). Torque is a useful 72 lb. ft. at 3000 rpm. This motor, although it's been around for some years, is the best thing about the Midget.

Smooth, responsive, and economical, it is.

Transmission is a four-speed with synchro on upper three ratios only. When will BMC introduce synchro on first to all its gearboxes? It's long overdue.

The gearchange is very good. Although the car had done less than 150 miles, there was none of the stiffness or baulkiness we've come to expect from BMC boxes.

The lever moved through the gate smoothly, and was absolutely no effort to use. Gearbox ratios are well chosen.

Comfortwise, the MG isn't really very different from the superseded Sprite. The seating position is low, and although the seats are reasonably comfortable you rely more on the doors than the seats to keep you located in vigorous cornering—and they get pretty hard after making contact with the shoulders a few times.

The steering wheel is too high set by today's standards and sitting behind the wheel is a strictly vintage sensation.

Instrumentation is reasonably comprehensive—speedo, tacho, fuel, water temperature, and oil pressure.

Retail price of the Midget hasn't been fixed yet, but when the Sprite went out of production it was selling for $2207. Bet your boots the MG will cost more than that. ●

50

AUTOCAR 10 April 1969

DESCRIPTION—MG MIDGET

It's harder than ever now to tell the Midget from the Sprite, as the chrome strip is no longer fitted down the centre of the MG bonnet. Both use a version of the BMC A-series engine with a capacity of 1,275 c.c. and developing 65 bhp net at 6,000 rpm. This is not the 1275S Mini-Cooper unit, which is more expensive and turns out 76 bhp.

The gearbox has a crash first gear and overall gearing is 15.4 mph per 1,000 rpm in top. Disc front brakes are 8.25in. dia. and there is no servo assistance. Rear drums are 7 x 1.25in.

Front suspension uses wishbones and coil springs with the arms of the dampers acting as upper wishbones. An anti-roll bar is optional; it was not fitted on the test car. At the rear half-elliptic leaf springs are used, with a live axle and lever-arm dampers. Steering is by rack and pinion.

Cross-ply Dunlop C41 tyres are the standard wear, on 3½in. rims and 13in. wheels. Optional wire wheels were fitted on the test car with the same size rims.

Performance—Midget

From rest, changing up at 6,500 rpm (of which more anon), the Midget reaches 50 mph in 9.5 sec and 60 mph in 13.8 sec. At the ¼-mile post, which is reached in 19.3 sec, the speed is exactly 70 mph. The recommended maximum engine speed is, in fact, 6,300 rpm. At these revs, the tachometer in the test car was indicating only 5,800 rpm and we therefore considered it in order to use this extra amount. The engine showed no signs of distress, but it is a sobering thought that an owner could unknowingly use 6,800 rpm!

DESCRIPTION—TRIUMPH SPITFIRE

The stylist "bone in its teeth" front bumper makes the MK 3 Spitfire, introduced in March 1967, easily distinguishable from its predecessors. Engine capacity went up from 1,147 c.c. to 1,296 c.c. at the same time. Peak power is now 75 bhp at 6,000 rpm.

Front discs are 9in. dia. and work without a servo; rear drums are 7 x 1.25in. The gearbox has standard Herald ratios and no syncromesh on bottom. Overall gearing is 15.8 mph per 1,000 rpm in direct top.

A separate chassis of basically cruciform shape is used. Front suspension is by means of double wishbones, in conjunction with coil springs, telescopic dampers and an anti-roll bar. At the rear, swing axles are used in conjunction with a transverse leaf spring. Longitudinal location is provided by a radius rod each side. Steering is by rack and pinion.

Standard tyres are 5.20-13in. Dunlop C41 cross-ply, mounted on 3.5in. pressed steel wheels. The test car was fitted with the optional 145-13in. Dunlop SP68 radial-ply tyres mounted on 4.5in. wire wheels. Amongst the other optional extras fitted were an overdrive, tonneau cover, heater, sun-vizors and auxiliary lamps.

The speedometer, on the other hand, over-reads by a modest 2.5 per cent, whilst the odometer is accurate. Maximum speed is 93 mph and the best one-way 94 mph. The latter represents 6,100 rpm—well over the 5,500 rpm (equivalent to 85 mph) recommended as the limit for continuous operation. With the hood down, the maximum speed drops to 88 mph.

It is almost impossible to resist the temptation to drive the Midget really hard. Certainly, this was its fate during the time it was in our hands. Yet, in the course of ordinary road

running, it returned as many as 34.8 mpg. Performance testing at MIRA, always a thirsty business, yielded only 26.4 mpg, but the average for the whole of the test period was a creditable 29.8 mpg. No measurable quantity of oil was used during the 800 miles we covered in the car.

Performance—Spitfire

The Spitfire's mechanical tachometer is much more accurate than the electronic type used in the Midget. At the maximum permissible engine speed of 6,500 rpm, it reads just under 6,400 rpm. Using this as the change point, 50 mph comes up from rest in 9.9 sec and 60 mph in 14.0 sec. The standing ½-mile takes 19.4 sec, 70 mph coming up just 0.1 sec later. We used the overdrive (an optional extra) when taking these figures, engaging it at 74 mph on third gear. As the maximum speed in overdrive is 92 mph, top gear was not required when taking the standing-start figures.

The speedometer over-reads by 5 per cent and the odometer by 3 per cent. Maximum speed, achieved in direct top, is 92 mph. The best one-way speed of 93 mph represents an engine speed of 5,900 rpm—just under the 6,000 rpm continuous-use limit. Engaging the overdrive third is 92 mph. Engaging the overdrive drops the speed by only 1 mph (down to 91 mph). The best one-way figure remains at 93 mph, but the revs are down to only 4,700 rpm. Lowering the hood reduces the maximum speed to 87 mph.

Despite hard driving, the Spitfire returned an overall petrol consumption figure of 31.3 mpg. The oil consumption, however, was less satisfactory, a pint being used every 250 miles or so.

2 CAR TEST
MG Midget Mk III
Triumph Spitfire Mk 3

NOJ 47F

Performance Differences

It would be difficult to find two more evenly matched cars. Their acceleration times differ by only a few tenths of a second and there is only 1 mph between their maximum speeds. Even lowering the hood has exactly the same effect on the maximum speed of both. The Spitfire has a slightly better petrol consumption, but this is offset by its considerable thirst for oil. Both offer approximately the same accommodation and are aimed at the same market. Yet they differ enormously in character.

The Midget is at its best when being hurled along a winding country road. Its beautifully light and precise gearchange encourages the enthusiastic driver to strive to get the best out of it and its low overall gearing merely adds to its nimbleness. The Spitfire, on the other hand, is a better proposition for long journeys on fast roads. Its higher gearing is an advantage under such conditions and its appeal can be further enhanced by specifying an overdrive.

Although the gearchange is so delightful on the Midget, the transmission is not without its shortcomings. All the indirect gears whine noticeably and the lever rattles quite badly at times. It also lacks syncromesh on first gear—an omission it shares with the Spitfire. The latter's gearbox, on the other hand, is very much quieter. Neither does the lever rattle but its travel, especially across the gate, is considerably greater and the change always feels a trifle "sticky".

The Midget has better spaced ratios but is only just able to re-start on a 1 in 3 gradient. With its lower first gear, the Spitfire copes with great ease.

In heavy traffic, the Midget is the pleasanter car to handle, despite its inferior visibility. This again is partially due to its better gearchange

Ultimate handling on the same bend at the same speed. The Midget (above) understeers safely on regardless while the Spitfire (below) jacks up at the rear and oversteers with power on

and lighter clutch. A more important factor is its better throttle response and cleaner carburation. The Spitfire has a marked tendency to surge at small throttle openings, especially at low speeds.

Ride and Handling—Midget

"Safety Fast" has long been an MG slogan and the Midget is a car that is really worthy of it. Chassis design is quite conventional and there is little to explain why the handling should be so outstanding. Good weight distribution and the use of a torsionally stiff monocoque body structure probably play a large part but some of it must be the result of careful suspension "tuning".

The little car feels ideally balanced. There is enough understeer to impart stability but not enough to cause embarrassment. The steering is very light and precise. One knows exactly what is happening at the front wheels, yet there is no unpleasant "fight". Response is instantaneous, yet the car doesn't feel in the least "twitchy". There is very little body roll and one has to try really hard to produce any signs of wheel-lifting. Most impressive of all is its incredibly forgiving nature. There can be precious few cars on the market with such inherently safe handling characteristics. Its only peculiarity is a tendency to veer to the right with power on and to the left with power off, but this is not even noticed after a while.

Such good handling qualities in a conventionally designed small car often involve ride penalties and the Midget is no exception. The ride is firm—almost choppy—over poor surfaces but the excellent seats effectively insulate the occupants. No matter how rough the going, the body structure gives an impression of absolute rigidity.

Ride and Handling—Spitfire

Our test car was equipped with 4.5in. wide wire wheels, shod with 145—13in Dunlop SP68 tyres—both optional extras. Past experience suggests that these make an appreciable contribution to the car's cornering capabilities and we found that it does handle very pleasantly indeed in all normal circumstances. Pushed hard enough, however, its basic swing-axle characteristics become very evident. The outer rear wheel suddenly tucks under, causing the tail-end to break away viciously. It must be emphasised that this only happens when cornering pretty hard and that reasonably prudent driving on public roads presents no problems. Although we have no wish to malign the reputation of this very pleasant sports car, we make no apology for referring to its handling limitations. Its stablemates, the GT6 and Vitesse, now have a completely redesigned rear suspension system. What a pity that the Spitfire has not been included.

The steering is rather low-geared, a feature that is emphasised by too large a steering wheel (16in dia.). As a result, response is not very rapid for a small sports car, but the effort is low and there is just the right amount of castor action. Straight-line stability is good and there is virtually no "fight", even on rough roads.

The ride is quite good but it suffers from considerable bump-thumping on rough roads and the body creaks a great deal. There is also a trace of scuttle shake. The result is that rough roads are heard and sensed, rather than felt.

Ride and Handling Differences

Driven moderately, there is really very little to choose between the handling of the two cars. The Midget has lighter and more responsive steering but the Spitfire has a slight edge in terms of directional stability.

Pushed to the limit, however, the Midget remains completely predictable and safe, whilst the Spitfire oversteers quite viciously. Although we acknowledge that it provides an alert driver with reasonable warning of its intentions, there is always the possibility of having to take sudden evasive action. In addition, it has been designed specifically to appeal to the sporting fraternity, many of whom, quite properly, enjoy driving at a brisker pace than average. We feel that the Spitfire doesn't provide the margin of safety they have a right to expect from a car of this type.

As far as ride is concerned, the Spitfire has the advantage. This is multiplied to some extent by the Midget's superior seats with their adjustable back-rests. Other features in favour of the Midget are the lower level of bump-thumping (possibly because it was fitted with cross-ply tyres) and the rigid feel of its body structure. The majority of people, however, clearly prefer the riding properties of the Spitfire.

Noise—Midget

The Midget suffers from wind noise especially around the top of the windscreen and wind-up windows. There is also flapping of the hood fabric against the hood irons at about 40 or 50 mph before wind pressure inside billows it out taunt.

Gearbox and transmission whine are very noticeable, especially in the intermediate gears, until they become drowned in the overall engine and wind roar, which also drowns speech from the radio however loud the volume. A harsh drive-line vibration sets up at speeds above an indicated 85 mph in the Midget, which cannot be passed and only gets progressively worse with speed.

Bad surfaces do little to transmit noise through the C41 tyres and awareness of road noise generally is absent other than tyre squeal caused by exuberant cornering.

Noise—Spitfire

The Spitfire is an extremely different story with tyre thump from indifferent surfaces coming through the radial tyres in a disturbing and very noisy way.

Loose stones thrown up against the underside by the tyres sounded like lead shot peppering the metal; some form of underseal would considerably reduce this. Also, under severe left-hand cornering, as the tyres sideslipped cum juddered on the road surface, a tremendous hammering came from the region of the gear lever housing showing that the engine-gearbox unit was making body contact somewhere in the bulkhead area.

When crossing washboard-like surfaces apparent scuttle shake added to the impression that more rattle was being generated than could actually be recognised. In spite of this, however, the Spitfire was far quieter for high speed cruising especially as overdrive reduced further the already lower level of engine and mechanical noise.

A bad exhaust boom comes in around 3,000 rpm in the Spitfire, but this passes away with increase in revs. A drive line vibration comes in at 85 mph with or without overdrive engaged.

Brakes

Both cars employ the front disc, rear drum brake arrangement, with both providing adequate braking power for moderate braking effort. Neither showed any tendency to lock-up prematurely under heavy braking, no pulling or

extreme fade under repeated application could be induced, the only apparent discomfort to the systems being some smoking of the Midget discs. This is not a fair criticism however, because the safer nature of the Midget led to its being driven harder for many more laps of the test course at MIRA, due to its fun appeal.

Fittings and Furniture
Spitfire

Seat adjustment was adequate to provide an almost straight arm driving position for a just short of 6ft driver, but the bucket back could not be altered for rake. With the seat well to the rear the release catch for the hinged backrest was all but inaccessible. The bucket back provides good sideways hold when cornering, but the comfort factor of the seat was not very high with little leg support. A rest for the left foot made the task of staying firmly in the seat somewhat easier.

The non-fly-off handbrake is located for easy use on the top of the transmission tunnel and the gear lever is nice and close to the wheel rim.

Gear positions are canted over towards the right and the steering wheel column slightly left to complete the 'twisted' set up, but acclimatization comes easily. The cockpit is carpeted and a kick-panel on the inside of the door is a good feature to avoid the muddy smears usually found on the inside of sports car doors. The door opening handle is located awkwardly near the door bottom but the window winder is sensibly placed and is free from the knuckle-barking obstacles. Small parcel shelves each side have open fronts.

Instruments are clustered centrally in a glossy wood facia panel making reading impossible without removing the left hand from its ten-to-two driving position. All the push pull or turn control knobs have their functions marked on them. The heating-ventilation system is effective, the steering column mounted lamp selector stalk includes a flasher and the overdrive stalk is on the right hand beyond the direction indicator stalk.

The hood is released by two levers from the windscreen to fold readily back into the space behind the seats once the securing studs around the base are released. A cover secures and protects the hood neatly in its stowed position.

Two levers on the bonnet sides allow forward hinging of the entire front to give very good access to the mechanicals. A smallish boot accommodating the spare wheel, will take the usual limited soft bag luggage.

Fittings and Furniture
Midget

A very comfortable seat provides excellent back and leg support with rake of the seat back adjustable. Forward leg room adjustment is restricted by the rear bulkhead so that a jackknifed, wheel-in-lap driving position is necessary for a tall person. Because of the support given by the seat however this cramped position surprisingly caused no discomfort at any time, and lateral hold is provided by the close proximity of the transmission tunnel and door. The gear lever is centrally placed on the hump of the transmission tunnel for very light fast gear changes. Foot controls include an organ throttle pedal and a dip switch cum left foot rest.

Difficult to find quickly without groping, the handbrake lever is situated on the passenger side of the transmission tunnel, and gets enveloped by a passenger. The three-spoked wheel affords a perfect view of the speedometer and rev counter which are angled towards the driver. The dashboard although old-fashioned in appearance is functionally efficient with all switches easily accessible. Heating-demisting

In the dark?

If it's on the subject
of sports cars for '62,
you'll find your hometown
BMC dealer ready, willing
and able to enlighten
you on them all.
Naturally, he'll boost one
of the BMC stable
of champions.
After you've test-driven one—
compared parts and service
facilities and warranties with
those of other makers—
we'll bet you will do some
boosting of your own.
See the light?

MG MIDGET
MGA 1600 Mk. II
AUSTIN HEALEY 3000 Mk. II
SPRITE

*Going abroad? Have a BMC car
meet you on arrival. Write for details.*

Products of **The British Motor Corporation, Ltd.**, makers of MG, Austin Healey, Sprite, Morris and Austin cars.
Represented in the United States by Hambro Automotive Corporation, 27 West 57th Street, New York 19, N. Y.

58

54

Above: With no front anti-roll bar, the Midget leans a lot in a corner, but remains stable and tidy right through. At the rear, the tyres are smoking from the sideways scrub

Right: Safety fast is the MG slogan, and speed holds no perils in the Midget. It is quick and tidy through corners always

controls are equally simple but efficient and opening quarterlights give fresh air at the expense of extra wind noise at speed. The bonnet release catch under the facia was very stiff on the test car and access to the engine compartment is reasonable.

The hood releases from the windscreen to fold back into the space behind the seats to be held in place by a neat cover. Erecting the hood needs quite some strength to clip it back into the windscreen and is a somewhat lengthy job.

Criticism must be levelled at the door opening catches, which are recessed high up near the rear edge and need considerable finger strength to operate.

Personal View

Choosing between two cars can sometimes be a difficult task. In this instance, however, there is absolutely no doubt in my mind.

The two are very similar in many ways, yet possess entirely different characters. Agility and excellent handling are the Midget's outstanding features, whilst effortless cruising, a more refined power train, rather more space and a better ride are the Spitfire's forte. There is one important point I must make clear at this stage —noise, especially wind noise, would deter one from buying a small sports car for long distance work. It would be primarily a fun machine. In this capacity I consider the Midget to be a far better proposition. Tweaking the engine—say to Cooper S standards—would make it even more fun.

It is only fair to record that my initial reactions were very different. I dislike the Midget driving position intensely and thought the power train (mainly the gearbox) lacked refinement. It still possesses these faults, of course, but I have grown to like the little car to such an extent that I am no longer aware of them. Never before have I undergone such a complete and rapid change of heart. DRT

Personal View

Choosing between the two cars in my case tends to avoid the main issue somewhat, because I find a pretty clear cut case for using

SPECIFICATION
MG
MIDGET

Maximum speeds		
rpm	**mph**	
6,050	93	Top
6,500	74	3rd
6,500	52	2nd
6,500	31	1st
		Acceleration
ind. mph	**sec**	**mph**
31	4.0	0-30
41	6.4	0-40
51	9.5	0-50
62	13.8	0-60
72	19.3	0-70
82	27.8	0-80
19.3 sec	70 mph	Standing ¼-mile
Top (4.22)	3rd (5.73)	**mph**
	8.5	10-30
10.8	6.7	20-40
10.0	6.7	30-50
10.5	7.4	40-60
12.9	9.6	50-70
18.2	—	60-80

29.8	**Overall mpg**
31	**Typical mpg**
Negligible consumption	**Oil— miles per pint**

FRONT ENGINE, REAR-WHEEL DRIVE

ENGINE
Cylinders	4, in line; 3 main bearings
Cooling system	Water; pump, fan and thermostat
Bore	70.6mm (2.78in.)
Stroke	81.3mm (3.20in.)
Displacement	1,275c.c. (77.8cu.in.)
Valve gear	Overhead; pushrods and rockers
Compression ratio	8.8-to-1 Min. octane rating: 99 RM
Carburettors	Twin SU HS2
Max. power	64bhp (net) at 5,800rpm
Max. torque	72lb.ft. (net) at 3,000rpm

TRANSMISSION
Gear ratios	Top 1.0
	Third 1.36
	Second 1.92
	First 3.20
	Reverse 4.12
Final drive	Hypoid bevel, 3.90-to-1

SUSPENSION
Front	Independent, coil springs, wishbones, Armstrong lever arm dampers
Rear	Live axle, half-elliptic leaf springs, Armstrong lever arm dampers.

STEERING
Type	Rack and pinion

BRAKES
Make and type	Lockheed discs front, drums rear, no servo
Dimensions	F. 8.25in. dia.; R. 7in. dia.; 1.25in. wide shoes

WHEELS
Type	Wire-spoked centre lock (extra). 3.50in. wide rim
Tyres—make	Dunlop
—type	C41 crossply tubeless
—size	5.20-13in.

SPECIFICATION

TRIUMPH SPITFIRE

Maximum speeds

	mph	rpm
Top	92	5,850
3rd	74	6,500
2nd	47	6,500
1st	27	6,500

Acceleration

mph	sec	ind. mph
0-30	4.5	31
0-40	6.9	41
0-50	9.9	51
0-60	14.0	62
0-70	19.5	72
0-80	27.8	83

Standing ¼-mile 70 mph 19.4 sec

mph	3rd (5.73)	Top (4.11)
10-30	7.8	
20-40	7.0	10.2
30-50	6.9	10.4
40-60	7.3	11.4
50-70	9.6	13.1
60-80	—	17.1

Overall mpg	31.3
Typical mpg	33
Oil— miles per pint	250

FRONT ENGINE, REAR-WHEEL DRIVE

ENGINE
Cylinders	4, in line; 3 main bearings
Cooling system	Water; pump, fan and thermostat
Bore	73.7mm (2.90in.)
Stroke	76mm (2.99in.)
Displacement	1,296c.c. (79.2cu.in.)
Valve gear	Overhead; pushrods and rockers
Compression ratio	9.0-to-1 Min. octane rating: 99 RM
Carburettors	Twin SU HS2
Max. power	75bhp (net) at 6,000rpm
Max. torque	75lb.ft. (net) at 4,000rpm

TRANSMISSION
Gear ratios	Top 1.0
	Third 1.39
	Second 2.16
	First 3.75
	Reverse 3.75
Final drive	Hypoid bevel, 4.11-to-1

SUSPENSION
Front	Independent, coil springs, wishbones, anti-roll bar, telescopic dampers
Rear	Independent, swing axles, transverse leaf spring, radius rods, telescopic dampers

STEERING
Type	Rack and pinion

BRAKES
Make and type	Girling discs front. drums rear, no servo
Dimensions	F. 9.0in. dia; R. 7in. dia.; 1.25in. wide shoes

WHEELS
Type	Wire spoked centre-lock (extra), 4.5in. wide rim
Tyres—make	Dunlop
—type	SP68 radial ply tubed
—size	145-13in.

Above: Whoops! Under full power the Spitfire swing axles eventually take over and flick the back out at the ultimate cornering speed

Left: What happens when there is more roll than wheel travel at the rear. As the outside wheel tucks under, tail end grip reduces

either car for a specific set of circumstances. If my journey was relatively short or around town or a blast of a distinctly sporting nature, then the Midget is the easy choice. Its solid feeling, compact and freely buzzing nature together with the gearbox which is a delight to snick around, tied with the utterly predictable handling, promises something which will not catch me out at an inconvenient moment. Its limitations however concern the very squashed but not cramped sitting position as my knees actually rest up against the underside of the dashboard. However the organ throttle pedal and the very comfortable seat with plenty of back support makes a journey very bearable. My main disappointment is the high noise level which discourages use of the Midget' on long motorway journeys. The ride is very firm and distinctly sporting with little noise to convey the hard work being put in by the tyres.

It should now be pretty obvious that my choice would be the Spitfire, if a lot of boring mileage had to be covered. Provided it is not driven in too sporting a fashion, it has remarkably long legs with little noise discomfort other than the harsh tyre thump present over rough surfaces. The overdrive does nothing to assist performance at all but makes life so much more pleasant. I did not find the creature comfort level to be very high due to the poor fit of the seat around my back, and the offset position of the pedals with the non-organ type throttle pedal. The instruments in the centre of the

dashboard which were completely obscured by my left hand did nothing to ease the physical discomfort caused by removing it every time a speed check became necessary.

There was nothing to choose between the brakes or the fresh air aspects of the two cars, although maybe the Spitfire hood was easier to stow and erect.

If the situation arose whereby one was to be mine, the two were side by side and I had one set of keys, the tyre dust would settle on the Spitfire as my Midget buzzed off.   CJH

PRICES

The price of the basic Midget, inclusive of Purchase Tax, is £768 13s 1d, with the heater now standard. The equivalent Spitfire costs £796 1s 5d, the heater accounting for £14 7s 3d.

The specification of the two test cars was very similar except that the Spitfire had an overdrive, sun visors and radial-ply tyres. Excluding these three items (the first two are not available for the Midget, in any case) the prices for the cars as tested are £849 12s 7d and £886 13s 0d, the Spitfire being the more expensive by £37 0s 5d. Note that these prices include a pair of safety belts at £6 10s 0d and a Radiomobile installation at £33 0s 0d, as well as the more usual extras like wire wheels and a tonneau cover. If overdrive is counted as well, the Spitfire goes up to £943 9s 1d, £93 16s 6d more than the Midget.

MG MIDGET 1275
COBURN IMPROVED

SMALL sports cars are fun, of that there can be no doubt—we have tried a few lately including standard MK3 Spitfire, standard 1275 Midget and even more fun a converted 1275 Midget, this is the one we are on about now. The Midget started life as a 1098 c.c. 1965 model and thus it stayed until those friendly men at Coburn improvements stuffed a 1275 go-unit and box into it. Not content with that they then made sure that the engine was a good one by carefully balancing the moving bits and lightening the flywheel. More urge still comes from the Janspeed exhaust manifold and 1½ in. S.U. carbs. We went and got the Midget from Coburn's at Hampstead (London) one fine and clear day—perfect sports car weather in fact; while we were waiting for the car to have service completed we had a little chat to Mike—whose in charge of the workshop side—and Fred Curtiss, their financial wizard. Both of them stressed that the car wasn't meant to be really hot, just a pleasant road car. Well they were vindicated both ways, 'cos the car went well enough to justify the absence of bumpers and the rather imposing power bulge on the bonnet, and yet was as flexible as the standard Spridget in town.

Quick we said—well we think 0–78 in 16.4 secs. is good going for a Midget, specially when you consider that the little car would pull 6500 in top on any straight worth the name! We had the feeling that given time it would pull a bit more than this—but we had to stick to a six five rev limit anyway. The only thing that disturbed us was the racket from the gearbox when in 4th travelling over 70 m.p.h. In fact, our test was to be cut short by trouble with the gearbox after doing the 0–70 acceleration run—we nearly cried. However we manfully fought off the urge and called it a day after working out that the Midget would pull 100 m.p.h. at 6500 r.p.m.

It's very nice having a reasonable amount of "go" under the bonnet of most cars, and it's even nicer having some "go" in a small sports machine. After all, that is what they're built for. In practical terms this means you can nip in and out of traffic at the drop of a hat—or your great hairy fat foot! As the Spridgets are quite small motors you'll probably find you can run the beast too.

Sometimes after our test it was discovered that Coburns had been supplied with a 948 c.c. Spridget gearbox which has the bronze bushes as opposed to the 1275s needle roller bearings—makes a big difference that!

In spite of these bothers we would like to thank Mr. Tony Wynter of Bexley, Kent, for letting us try his Midget.

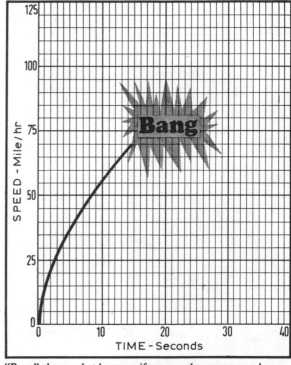

"Bang" shows what happens if you use the wrong gear box.

MG midget
what's in a name?

FIRST impressions CAN be misleading. Last month when we had a brief exploratory run in BMC's new baby MG — the Midget — we weren't too impressed.

We felt then that it had a vintage feel about it — almost as if it was a reincarnation of some earlier MG. The steering wheel is too big, and too close to the operator's chest, the ride is overly firm, without the suppleness we've come to expect of modern sportscars, and the handling was, to say the least, most unsporty.

None of these things have changed. But after spending a week with ESK 290, we find them not nearly as hard to live with as we had imagined they would be.

What wasn't obvious when we first drove the car was the tremendous revvability of the motor, and the quite good performance it offered. With only a few miles up the car was of course very stiff, and completely lacking in the flexibility we found so enjoyable when we drove it later.

What's new?

Basically, the Midget is just the Austin Healey Sprite with the name changed. BMC found that the magic of the octagonal MG nameplate was attracting buyers — the MGB is the country's best-selling sports-car, despite a price tag considerably in excess of the Sprite, Honda and Spitfire.

So they did the obvious thing, phasing out the Sprite in the second half of 1967 and introducing the MG Midget in early 1968.

Most important single difference between the two cars lies in the engine compartment. The Sprite used a tuned 1098 cc. motor and it produceu 59 bhp at 5750 rpm and 65 lb. ft. of torque at 3500 rpm.

The Midget uses a 1275 cc. motor — basically the Mini Cooper S unit but detuned to the extent of smaller valves and a milder camshaft — which produces 65 bhp at 6000 rpm and 72 lb. ft. of torque at 3000 rpm. Compression ratio is slightly down from 8.9 to 8.8 to 1.

The Sprite was never a difficult car to drive in traffic. It's light weight and the flexibility of the 1100 motor were sufficient to allow it to potter along with the best of the family sedans. Imagine then how much better the Midget is with considerably more torque developed at lower rpm.

It's a great potterer — at the same time having a good reserve of performance on tap, irrespective of the gear ratio used.

Speaking of gear ratios brings us to a piece of news that will definitely interest potential Midget buyers. If they haven't already done so, BMC will shortly fit synchromesh to first gear.

That will be an improvement, although we never had difficulty engaging first on the move — either by double declutching, or just gritting our teeth and crunching it in.

Part of the Midget's flexibility is no doubt due to a final drive ratio which many critics feel is too low. The Midget's tachometer is red-lined at 6300 rpm but the 4.22 final drive ratio allows the car to run to 7000 rpm in top without any trouble at all. That gives it an outright top speed of 107 mph — because it is geared to do 15.5 mph/1000 rpm.

We did the right thing though and backed-off the throttle on our top speed runs, going through the traps with the tacho on the red line. This gave us 93.7 mph in both directions.

If you chose to ignore the red line, the Midget's top speed is a fair and

square 107. Incidentally, BMC say the motor is capable of standing 7000 rpm without breaking to pieces.

Appointments

Like the Sprite that's gone before, the Midget offers pretty reasonable comfort for two people.

The seats are pleasant to sit on — more so, we think, than the Sprite's — although they look the same. They don't provide that hip-hugging support essential for ultimate comfort at speed, but by wedging oneself against the door and seatback and belting up with the standard seatbelt it is possible to stay firmly located.

The cabin area is fully carpeted, and a handy shelf behind the rear seats is also nicely trimmed with carpet. A good feature of this shelf area is that it is not made completely useless when

Sprite replacement turns out a much better car than we had at first expected

MG midget

the hood is stowed. With the top down, there is still room for a considerable amount of soft luggage in addition to that area provided in the miniscule boot.

The Midget's hood is a considerable refinement over the Sprite's — not so much in the mechanics of erecting and lowering as in mode of stowage.

Once it is folded up, it can be neatly hidden under a half tonneau — and, as we've already said, it doesn't seriously interfere with stowage.

Visibility is not brilliant in any direction, but this is not unusual in sports-cars. The windscreen is rather low, and the mini wipers sweep only a small area.

Handling, brakes

The Midget is a very strong under-steerer, and while we appreciate that this feature makes it a safe vehicle for the young and somewhat in-experienced drivers who will buy it, it is not the least sporty.

The color action pictures of the MG show BMC rally ace Evan Green at the wheel. Despite his considerable skill and daring, he just wasn't able to induce a tail-out oversteer attitude at any stage of our photographic sessions, and he tried handbrake turns and all!

We subsequently pumped the front tyres (Dunlop SP41 radials are standard) up to 30 psi and this reduced the understeer quite a bit.

On dirt roads, of course, the tail hangs out. Acceleration on loose surfaces causes the rigid rear axle to tramp and dither, and on very rough sections the front tyres chafe on the wheel arches.

Steering is rack and pinion, and very direct at 2.3 turns lock to lock. Sharp and sensitive on good surfaces, it produces a lot of feedback and chatter on poor roads. A touch more self-centring would help, too.

One of the Midget's most outstanding features is its superb braking ability. It is one of only two cars we've so far subjected to our crash braking test that has recorded a full 1g stop. And it did this not once but twice in succession. See our performance panel for more details.

The Dunlops SP41s, which have a legendary reputation for stickiness, are obviously contributing considerably to the Midget's braking.

Performance

We've already talked at some length about the Midget's top speed. Acceleration is most respectable. The car ran a best S.S. ¼-mile of 18.8 sec. and averaged 18.9, and accelerated to 60 in 12.5 sec.

Mid-range acceleration is good. The car's flexibility is such that it will run along on a whiff of throttle and take off strongly when the throttle is opened.

The average owner could expect 33-34 mpg. We achieved this in our normal running around, dropped the consumption to 27 when we did our performance runs. The six-gallon fuel tank is totally inadequate.

There's nothing really new about the MG Midget except the name — it's a collection of bits with which we're all pretty familiar. However, it's a mixture that blends well, and one that is easy to like.

We like it — despite our earlier misgivings. We're sure young sports-car enthusiasts will like it, too. ●

Manufacturer: BMC (Aust.) Pty. Ltd., Zetland, Sydney.
Test car supplied by them.
Price as tested: $2480.

SPECIFICATIONS

ENGINE
Water cooled, four cylinders in line, cast iron block, three main bearings.

Bore x stroke	70.6 x 81.2 mm.
Capacity	1275 cc. (77.9 cu. in.)
Compression	8.8 to 1
Carburettor	Twin SUs
Fuel pump	Electrical
Fuel tank	6 gallons
Fuel recommended	super
Valve gear	pushrod ohv
Max. power (gross)	65 bhp at 6000 rpm
Max. torque	72 lb./ft. at 3000 rpm
Specific power output	51 bhp/litre
Electrical system	12v, 43 amp hr. battery

TRANSMISSION
Four-speed manual with synchro on upper three ratios. Single dry plate clutch.

Gear	Ratio	Mph/1000 rpm	Max. mph
1st	3.2	5.0	30 (6000)
2nd	1.916	8.3	50 (6000)
3rd	1.257	11.6	70 (6000)
4th	1.00	15.5	98 (6300)
Final drive ratio			4.22 to 1

CHASSIS

Wheelbase	6ft. 8in.
Track front	3ft. 10½in.
Track rear	3ft. 8¾in.
Length	11ft. 5in.
Width	4ft. 6½in.
Height	4ft. 1in.
Clearance	5in.
Kerb weight	14 cwt. 35 lb.
Weight distribution front/rear	52.4/47.6%

SUSPENSION
Front: Independent by coils and wishbones, with tubular shock absorbers.
Rear: Rigid axle with semi-elliptic leaf springs and tubular shock absorbers.

Brakes:	8½in. disc, 7in. drum. 190 sq. in. of swept area.
Steering	Rack and pinion
Turns lock to lock	2-1/3
Turning circle	32ft.

Wheels: Knock-off wire with 5.20 by 13 tubeless radial tyres.

PERFORMANCE

Top speed	94.1 mph
Average (both ways)	93.7 mph
Standing quarter-mile	18.9 sec.

Acceleration

Zero to		seconds
30 mph		3.7
40 mph		6.0
50 mph		9.0
60 mph		12.5
70 mph		16.5
80 mph		25.1

	3rd	top
20-40 mph	5.7	—
30-50 mph	5.5	8.0
40-60 mph	6.3	7.4
50-70 mph	6.7	7.7

BRAKING: Ten crash stops from 60 mph.

Stop	percent G	pedal pressure
1	95	80 lb.
2	100	90 lb.
3	100	100 lb.
4	95	95 lb.
5	95	95 lb.
6	95	100 lb.
7	90	105 lb.
8	85	110 lb.
9	80	110 lb.
10	80	120 lb.

Comments: Rear brake lock-up on stops 4 and 5.
Consumption: 27 mpg over 112 miles, including all tests; 34.1 mpg in normal country and suburban use.
Speedo error:

Indicated mph	30	40	50	60	70	80
Actual mph	28.1	37.8	47.4	56.4	66.1	75.2

BLMC Sports Cars

Exterior styling and interior trim changes only for 1970 Sprite and MGs; no changes to mechanical specification. Prices up.

THE BLMC factory at Abingdon, the biggest one in the world devoted solely to the production of sports cars, will suffer little disruption of schedules as a result of the introduction of the 1970 models of the MGB, MG Midget and Austin-Healey Sprite.

Changes in all three cars are confined to interior trim and exterior finish and fittings. Mechanically they continue entirely unchanged; basically, the cars follow the trend towards greater comfort and luxury in this type of vehicle.

Exterior alterations to both the small and medium-sized cars are very similar. All three have new matt-black grilles, twin rear bumpers with the number plate between them, and Rostyle wheels. The Sprite and Midget also have matt black lower side panels carrying the name of the car. The BLMC corporate badge makes an appearance on the front wings of each car.

Cross-ply tyres are still standard; radial-ply tyres and wire-spoke wheels are options. Auto-

NEW FOR 1969/70

matic transmission continues as an option on the MGB and MGB GT.

A new feature of all three interiors is the provision of fully-adjustable reclining seats. The dashboards have been redesigned to improve safety still further, and now incorporate rocker-type switches. The interiors of the smaller cars are now fully carpeted, and a gear-lever gaiter is fitted.

As far as prices are concerned, the Midget costs exactly the same as the Sprite for the first time in its life; previously, it has always cost slightly more. Both models are now £818. The MGB is now £1,125, and the MGB GT £1,254.

The colour range for 1970 is all-new, except for the retention of British Racing Green. There are four other colours (shared with the new Mini Clubman and 1300GT ranges); glacier white, blue royale, flame red and bronze yellow. Interiors are in black only.

The MGB roadster has changed in parallel with the GT. Note the Rostyle wheels which are now standard; wire wheels continue as an option

From the front, the latest MGB GT is recognizable by the new matt-black grille. This car is fitted with radial-ply tyres, but cross-plies are standard

Seen here at the Press introduction, the Sprite and the Midget now differ only in badges; everything else—including price—is identical. Recognition points on the 1970 cars include the matt-black windscreen surrounds and lower side panels. The grille layout is new

Chapter Twelve in the continuing story of...

THE MIGHTY SPRIDGET

Defying the principles of planned obsolescence, the 1970 Midget stands as a permanent sporting fixture in a rapidly changing automotive scene. John Crawford goes on marathon test to determine this veteran's life expectancy.

THE Midget/Sprite, or as it's known in the trade the Spridget, has been around close on 12 years. The basic car hasn't changed all that much, but owners of early cars would have to drive the current BLMC offering to see how far things have progressed.

In 1958, BMC released a low priced fun car called the Sprite. It was intended to be a bit on the revolutionary side, incorporating a few new design features such as retractable headlights, but after doing its sums, the marketing team found the concept was moving quickly out of the low-priced field.

Obviously, the revolutionary bits had to be dropped.

The 1970 MG Midget isn't all that revolutionary, in fact compared with current design, it is pretty old hat. But, BLMC has been in the car business long enough to know you don't bite off the hand that feeds you. The Spridget has been, and still is, a big money earner for the Corporation and there's no sense in doing a drastic re-work and pricing yourself out of the market. The Spridget is tried and true and is still really the only reasonably priced, genuine sports/fun car available.

Far Left: Midget in technicolor and wide-view. New Mark Two has detail grille restyle and some other detail touch-ups, but there are more under-the-skin changes.

Above Left: Back sill panels and reversing lights are worthy dress-up and function extras to mark the new Mark Two.

The Midget hasn't gone the way of its older brother, the "Boulevarde B". Certain concessions have been made in the interests of comfort and, most importantly, competition — not so much racing type competition, but market type. The Midget has been popular in Britain and Australia, but its success on the American sales graph was the clincher that led BLMC to update its baby in much the same way as European car makers have done when their cars have faced US opposition.

During its 12 years, the Spridget's major changes have been a slightly different body, disc front brakes, new motor and an improved convertible type hood. Other changes have mostly been details — important to the overall improvement, but still minor. The Spridget, the best selling sports car on the Australian market, still manages to do well overseas, despite the number of competitors in its price and specification range.

The secret of this tremendous success must lie in the fact that the Midget is a very honest motor car. It doesn't pretend to be anything more than it is. The car still has some annoying shortcomings, but, at this stage, the only thing that would improve the car further is a completely new design.

The MG Midget sells in Australia for $2643, quite a bit more than when the car was originally introduced (even allowing for cost-of-living increases). It has also progressed greatly.

THE MIGHTY SPRIDGET

The changes over the first Midget (or the fifth Sprite if you wish) are new seats (adjustable for rake), padded leather-covered steering wheel, rear bumperettes instead (of full width bumper bar), reversing lights, blacked out sill panels, new grille and the new one-hand operated hood.

The engine and transmission unit remains unchanged and, departing from the parent plant policy, BLMC in Australia offers wire wheels as standard. In Britain, Midget owners get steel disc wheels with Rostyle type wheel covers (same as Triumph 2.5 PI).

The new seats are great. The adjustment provides enough movement to suit most drivers, particularly the girls. New padding makes them pleasant to sit on, but BLMC (in line with what we think must be British car makers' general policy) still persists in putting those annoying little seat adjusters on its products. The Japanese and Continentals (even Americans) provide a prominent cranked lever with a large plastic knob on the end, and its about time British Leyland spread the change through its entire model range.

The leather-padded steering wheel is good to hold and after driving the car for a while you begin to wonder why this sort of extra wasn't added long ago. But on the Midget, this fitting does cause problems. With the plastic wheel (early cars had plastic spokes, later cars wire spokes) you could always see the instruments, but now, apart from arranging the wheel in a sympathetic position, or aiming your eyesight through the drilled holes in the spokes, it is damn near impossible to see the cluster and practically dangerous to look at if you are driving at speed. Short of re-shaping the angle of the spokes there isn't a quick, cheap way out.

BLMC has added a multi-purpose stalk (flashers, high-beam, horn, headlamp flasher) to the right hand side of the steering column and this also gets all hung up with the steering wheel. The multi-purpose stalk seems closer to the wheel than the blinker-only wand it replaces and with your hands firmly gripping the steering wheel the stalk is easy to bump and occasionally hard to use. The main problem is that the wheel itself is a larger diameter than the plastic ones it replaces. The increased diameter is probably cheaper because the same wheel is used for the Midget and MGB. The "B" requires a large steering wheel to reduce steering effort — the Midget doesn't.

However, steering through the rack and pinion is still light and positive on the Midget and with almost three turns lock to lock, only a small movement is needed to send it off on a new path.

Still on debit points, the test Midget had a badly fitted boot lid. On reflection, gappy, ill-fitting boot lids have always been a Sprite trademark. The hood fitted tightly, but after a couple of ups and downs a sudden draught developed. We tried raising and lowering the hood a couple of more times, but

Mag-alloy wheel options on this English Spridget don't make local sense because of standard wire centre-locks. British car has standard disc wheels.

couldn't solve the problem. Together with hood flap, we suffered a steady three knot gale over our legs. Then the rains came — inside the car as well as outside. BLMC assured us Midget hoods normally fit snugly and claimed this unit had seen a hard life. We still feel the hood needs improvement.

British Leyland shows a standard heater-demister on its brochures for the Midget, but this is not fitted in Australia, due to a problem with the CKD packs from England. B-L Australia ordered its basic packs from Britain with the heater-demister included and, on assurance from the parent company, printed its brochures and publicity material. The CKD packs arrived on the wharves without the heater units and British Leyland put the car on the market here without them. The cars will have heaters fitted by January 1971 (compulsory, anyway, under Australian safety design rules) and there will be a slight price adjustment. If you want a heater now go see your friendly B-L dealer who can give you details of the rather finicky conversion. Alternatively, national heater firms may help out.

The little car is easy to ventilate, however, if you're travelling with the hood raised because of the underdash vent and quarter lights, plus the wind-up windows. One benefit of the new hood arrangement is that you no longer have to stow the hood in the boot. It folds up neatly around the rear of the passenger compartment and has a storage tonneau built-in. This neatly flips over the folded top and fastens to the back wall of the bathtub. The boot space saved is still obstructed by the spare wheel lying flat on the floor, but that can't be improved without major structural alterations.

With a bit of juggling, it is surprising how much you can fit into the small capacity compartment - particularly soft luggage. Spridget owners will notice one interior change — the loss of the metal surround for the gear lever. This was nearly a traditional part of the design, but it has been replaced by an attractive stitched vinyl glove. This feature may also cut down noise from the transmission.

The test car had a little backlash from the differential and the gearbox did give out a few groans, but after a week in the car it is obvious BLMC engineers have tried to quieten it. With extra soundproofing and an extra muffler, the car sounds quite subdued, but when you wind it up there is enough noise to let you know that everything is working.

Performance on the MG Midget MK, Two is unchanged from that of the previous model. It performs well and is quite reliable, but a few more horses would help. The Spridget's big feature over the years has been its chuck-about-ability. This is a point raised many times over the years in road tests of the Sprite/Midget, but one which is an endearing quality.

MG Midget 1970-71 vintage can be picked by new grille treatment, black sill panels. Australian Midgets get centre-lock wires as standard equipment — English versions get discs.

It is a real fun car, a great first car for the young driver and it has good enough road manners to forgive the uninitiated. It is no wonder that Sprite/Midget owners start modifying their cars. The Midget has such forgiving handling qualities and responds so well to extra tuning that even after the initial joy of owning and driving you can practically make a different car of it and start enjoying the car all over again.

The Sprite was always a safe understeerer. The car was easy enough to provoke into a tail-out attitude and the original suspension set-up lasted until the Mark Three. Front suspension featured coils and wishbones with quarter elliptics and live axle at the rear — lever action shockers all round. With the Mark three, came a change in the rear suspension, and semi-elliptics made the ride better at the expense of a little more understeer.

The next handling and suspension change came with the official factory fitting of a front anti-roll bar. Sprite owners had been fitting this accessory themselves for some time and they were a must on racing Sprites. BLMC included them in the specifications and price only on the first Midget.

Sprite brakes have always been adequate for the job but before WHEELS got down to recording some braking figures, the stoppers on the test car seemed a bit spongy. As the figures on the performance panel show, the brakes performed well. With 8½ in. discs on the front and 7 in. drums on the rear the car pulled up straight from a 60 mph panic stop.

Controls generally are light, the clutch gives the impression it will stand up well to fast starts and changes and the gearbox ratios seem well enough spaced for good performance (more about ratios in a moment). However the gearbox had two failings, one not previously noticed on Spridgets before. Firstly, there is still no first gear syncro, but more importantly the change from second to third was diabolical.

During our test with many different and competent drivers we continually suffered missed changes and often snicked first on the way through. The driver really has to concentrate hard for a clean change because a close gate and lack of spring protection, slides the lever into first instead of third.

According to the brochures, the gearbox is a close ratio one, but inspection reveals the ratios are in fact unchanged. There is a close ratio box for the Midget, but unfortunately it isn't available as an optional extra (only through the special tuning department at Abingdon).

The Midget Mark Two engine is unchanged and is the rugged and reliable 1275 cc S-type unit. The important features of this block over previous A-series units are: Larger main and big end bearings, increased capacity combustion chambers, bigger valves and improved cooling passages. The advertised horsepower is 65 bhp produced at 6000 rpm, but the obvious feature of the powerplant is the generous (relatively) amount of torque available. This makes the car an easy handler round town and, of course, helps the car's cruising ability and fuel consumption figures.

Although the tacho is redlined from 6400 and peak power is developed at 6000 the engine puts up a vocal complaint when pushed over 5500. It still

New interior is marked by new seats, leather-alloy wheel, and vinyl boot for the gearlever extension.

operates well in the high rev range and, despite what sounds like valves bouncing off pistons, the engine will run right up to seven grand (although it runs out of breath long before that). The oil pressure and water temperature remained constant throughout the test.

The Midget engine is still fed by 1¼ in. SUs. The car cruises well, if a little noisily, at around 75-80. The speedometer accuracy was in question all the way up the range. Over 60 mph the readings became increasingly optimistic with the meter reading 100 mph at 6000 (actual speed 95).

One other gauge which Midget owners must learn to watch is the fuel contents. WHEELS recorded an overall consumption figure on test of 30 mph but the tank holds only a miserable six gallons and the needle seems to drop very quickly. A larger tank is necessary, but here we get back to basic design problems and, short of a new rear end redesign, there is sufficient room to instal a larger fuel tank.

The Midget seems to have its section of the sports car market to itself, but the car doesn't compete with some of the sports sedans now on the market, especially those from Japan, in terms of equipment and value for money.

Its success is its sporting concept — one which enthusiasts find highly acceptable. It is a strange anomaly in the automotive world that sports cars gain wide market acceptance, with lower value-for-money standards than would be acceptable for any sedan or sporting coupe.

This situation has lasted for years and shows no sign of winding up. British Leyland certainly doesn't have an alternative for the Midget planned — so it could be with us in similar form for quite a while yet. Give it at least three years.

TECHNICAL DETAILS OVER THE PAGE

wheels ROAD TEST

TECHNICAL DETAILS

MAKE: . . . . MG
BODY TYPE: . . . . Two-seater sports
OPTIONS: . . . . .radio
MILEAGE START: 5400
WEIGHT: . . . .(714 kgm) 1575 lb
MODEL: . . . . MIDGET
PRICE: $2643
COLOR: . . . . .Mustard yellow
MILEAGE FINISH: 5604

FUEL CONSUMPTION:
Overall . . . . 28 mpg
Cruising . . . . 30 mpg

TEST CONDITIONS:
Weather . . . . .dry
Surface . . . . .bitumen
Load . . . . 2 persons
Fuel . . . . super

SPEEDOMETER ERROR (mph):

Indicated	30	40	50	60	70	80	90
Actual	28	38	47	56	65	75	84

PERFORMANCE

Piston speed at max bhp . . . . .(970 m/min) 3200 ft/min
Top gear mph per 1000 rpm . . . . 16.1 mph per 1000
Engine rpm at max speed 6200
Lbs (laden) per gross bhp (power-to-weight) 26 lb per 65 bhp

MAXIMUM SPEEDS:
Fastest run . . . .(148 kph) 92 mph
Average of all runs . . . .(138 kph) 86 mph
Speedometer indication, fastest run . . . .(156 kph) 98 mph

IN GEARS:
1st . . . . (48 kph) 30 mph 5500 rpm
2nd . . . . (80 kph) 50 mph 5500 rpm
3rd . . . .(112 kph) 70 mph 5500 rpm
4th . . . .(138 kph) 86 mph 5500 rpm

ACCELERATION THROUGH GEARS WITH CHANGE POINTS

STANDING 1/4 MILE 18·7

4TH 86MPH
3RD 70MPH
2ND 50MPH
IST 30MPH

TOP SPEED 86 M.P.H.

MPH ELAPSED TIME IN SECONDS

ACCELERATION (through gears):
0-30 mph . . . . 3.4 secs
0-40 mph . . . . 5.5 secs
0-50 mph . . . . 7.9 secs
0-60 mph . . . . 11.0 secs
0-70 mph . . . . 14.9 secs
0-80 mph . . . . 20.8 secs

	2nd gear	3rd gear	4th gear
20-40 mph	3.9 sec	5.9 sec	8.6 sec
30-50 mph.	4.4 sec	5.5 sec	8.5 sec
40-60 mph	3.0 sec	5.8 sec	8.0 sec
50-70 mph	—	7.2 sec	8.6 sec

STANDING QUARTER MILE:
Fastest run . . . . 18.7 secs
Average all runs . . . . 18.7 secs

BRAKING:
From 30 mph to 0 . . . . .1.9 secs
From 60 mph to 0 . . . . .3.4 secs

ENGINE:
Cylinders . . . . .Four
Bore and Stroke . (70.61 mm) 2.78 in. x (81.28 mm) 3.2 in.
Cubic Capacity . . . . (1275 cc) 77.9 cu in.
Compression Ratio 8.8:1
Valves . . . . pushrod overhead
Carburettors . . . . . twin SU-type HS.2 semi-downdraught
Fuel Pump . . . . SU electric
Oil Filter . . . . .full flow
Power at rpm . . . . .65 bhp @ 6000
Torque at rpm . . . . (10.9 kg/m) 72 lb/ft @ 3000

TRANSMISSION:
Type . . . . four speed, syncro on 2nd, 3rd, 4th
Clutch:
  (16 cm) 6.5 in. diaphragm spring hydraulically operated.
Gear lever location . . . . .centre floor
Ratios:

	Overall	Direct
1st	12.5	3.2
2nd	7.5	1.9
3rd	5.3	1.4
4th	3.9	1.0
Final Drive	3.9 to 1	

CHASSIS AND RUNNING GEAR:
Construction . . . . .Monocoque
Suspension front . . . . . . Coils, upper and lower wishbones
Suspension rear . . . . . . Semi-elliptical and live rear axle
Shock absorbers . . . . Lever action
Steering type . . . . Rack and pinion
Turns I to I 2¼
Turning circle . . . . (8.4 m) 32 ft
Steering wheel diameter . . . . (39 cm) 15½ in.
Brakes type . . . . Front disc, rear drum
Dimensions . . . .(20.9 cm) 8.25 in. x (17.8 cm) 7 in.

DIMENSIONS:
Wheelbase . . . . (203 cm) 80 in.
Track front . . . . (118 cm) 46.3 in.
Track rear . . . . (116 cm) 45.3 in.
Length . . . .(350 cm) 137.4 in.
Height . . . . (124 cm) 48.6 in.
Width . . . . (140 cm) 54.9 in.
Fuel Tank Capacity . . . .(27.3 litres) 6 galls

TYRES:
Size . . . . 145 x 13
Pressures . . . . (2.65 kg/m) 30 lb/sq in. x
  (1.95 kg/m) 28 lb/sq in.
Make on test car . . . . Dunlop

GROUND CLEARANCE:
Registered . . . . (12.7 cm) 5 in.

MIDGET MK3 1275

IN BASIC form the MG Midget costs £736, which makes it the cheapest manufacturer's sports car on the market, bar its badge brother, the Sprite, at £724. Both are fun to drive and surprisingly civilised, though very noisy to cruise at 70 or over. With the wind-up windows and foldaway hood there's plenty of comfort even in pouring rain. The best way to enjoy a Midget is obviously with the hood down, when you can still reach 90 m.p.h. and appreciate what the pilots of those WW1 biplanes felt! The quick and accurate rack-and-pinion steering, combined with the complete dependability of the handling, make this one of the faster ways of travelling across this traffic-infested island. Acceleration isn't fantastic, with 0-60 in 12·0 secs—but combined with a wide and quite torquey power band there's very little that can actually cover ground more speedily, or more enjoyably.

Mechanically, Spridgets now have a stronger cog box and 1275 c.c. to help fend off Spitfire and S800 competition. As we all should know, this 1275 isn't such a close brother to the 'S' unit as many would wish; still, it puts out 65 horses (six more than the 1098s) and 72 lb. ft. of torque—which is 10 lb. ft. increase over the old model. Compression ratio is 8·8:1—so we used a blend of five and four star fuel on which it was quite content to trundle for just over 30 miles before demanding refreshment; we used no oil at all in over 1,000 miles.

Driving position is still of the hunched-back-and-nose-pressed-against-the-horn-boss variety, hell on earth for a six-footer. The seats offend too, being of a similar design to the MGB's and giving minimal side support—and that's something you need in a hard-driven Spridget.

Considering how little rubber it has on the road (3·5 D rims shod with C41's as standard) the car holds onto the road quite well, but in the wet controlled sliding takes over. Driving a Spridget for a short distance in rain is entertaining, but over a long distance one soon gets fed up with the poor forward vision enforced by the small screen; policemen can hide unobserved behind, too! With the soft top up the engine and rear axle noise become much more obvious,

and it takes a hardy passenger to endure a constant 70 m.p.h.—especially when she can't hear her favourite song above 65!

And if you can't hear a Radiomobile, then believe us it's getting noisy in there.

The gearbox is just right, with its short lever and light, prompt action. Now that so many cars have an all-synchromesh box, we did find ourselves cursing the lack of this useful item on first though. Unlike some of our contemporaries, we found that it took some time to get first slot without some 'orrible grindings. Ratios are well spaced, returning 29, 49 and 69 m.p.h. in the first three at 6,000 r.p.m. Third is a really useful cog, taking you past main road traffic in fine style. Once on the move we usually didn't use second unless at a standstill.

We were disappointed to find that the heater is still an optional extra and that even then it doesn't provide enough warmth for winter conditions—ventilation is no problem, unless it's wet, when the interior is liable to steam up. On second thoughts that might well be a plus point with you Casanova types....

Ach so, Spridgets are still good value for money and real fun to conduct. Surely BLMC could alter the seating position and bung in radials, heater and headlamp flasher at this price though?

PERFORMANCE

m.p.h.	secs.
0–30	4·0
0–40	6·1
0–50	8·4
0–60	12·2
0–70	18·1
0–80	26·8

Top speed (best) 98 m.p.h.
Top speed (mean of two ways) 96·1 m.p.h.
Price as tested £784.
Overall m.p.g. 32

Not the same as the Cooper 'S', but definitely a 1275, rocker cover an' all.

AUTOTEST
MG MIDGET MK III
(1,275 c.c.)

AT-A-GLANCE: BLMC's familiar small sports-car in latest paintwork and trim, with some detail improvements. Higher gearing increases top speed slightly but not acceleration. Excellent handling, firm ride, good value and good fun.

MANUFACTURER

British Leyland Motor Corporation Ltd., (MG Division), Abingdon-on-Thames, Berkshire.

PRICES

Basic	£692	0s	0d
Purchase Tax	£213	14s	9d
Seat belts (approx.)	£10	0s	0d
Total (in G.B.)	£915	14s	9d

EXTRAS (inc P.T.)

*Tonneau cover and rail	£11	15s	0d
*Radial ply tyres	£9	2s	9d
Wire wheels	£32	12s	9d
Oil cooler	£13	1s	1d
Anti-roll bar	£3	18s	4d
Hard top	£65	5s	7d
Headrests (pair)	£10	8s	1d

*Fitted to test car

PRICE AS TESTED £936 12s 6d

PERFORMANCE SUMMARY

Mean maximum speed	94 mph
Standing start ¼-mile	19.6 sec
0-60 mph	14.1 sec
30-70 mph through gears	15.8 sec
Typical fuel consumption	30 mpg
Miles per tankful	180

THERE are, surprisingly, still too few contenders for the role of the young man's (or young woman's) first sports-car. With still-steeper insurance one might have thought that the demand for a proper open two-seater of acceptably nippy performance, nimble handling, sports-car appointments and—by today's inflated standards—middling low price, was bigger than ever. At £906 Austin-Healey Sprite-cum-MG Midget in its latest form still remains perhaps the best car of the type available. Performance, though good, is still not as good as a number of saloon cars, but the Midget (which is the "badge" we tested) is undeniably a true sports-car.

The body shape dates back to 1961 when the highly distinctive "frog-eyed" Sprite was restyled to a more conventional—and perhaps less original—shape. Later, a more important change in one way, the unusual quarter-elliptic leaf-sprung back axle was altered to ordinary half-elliptic springing which more or less eliminated the car's marked and—once you'd got to know it—amusing tendency to slight rear-axle steer. The faithful BMC A-series engine fitted has gradually gone up in capacity and power; it stands now at 1,275 c.c. in the inexplicably mild 64 bhp at 5,800 rpm form. (Its saloon stablemate the MG1300 Mk II is allowed 5 bhp more and is at some points slightly faster.) Most recent alterations are a 3.9-to-1 final drive (in place of 4.22), black paint on the sills giving the effect of particularly heavy side-flashes, the words "Midget" in heavy chrome also on the sides, nave-plateless wheels (wire-wheels remaining an option), and self-propping boot and bonnet stays (at last).

From the performance point of view, the gearing change is the most important, the overall figure going up from 15.4 to 16.5 mph per 1,000 rpm on the Michelin ZX 145 SR-13in. radial-ply tyres on the test car (cross-ply tyres are standard). (Owners with other tyres fitted should note that in this particular size there are different rev-per-mile figures for the various makes, giving different overall gearing.) Previously the same-size Midget's top speed of 93 mph was seen after peak-power engine speed—6,000 rpm—but the higher-geared test car achieved 94 mph mean at 5,700 rpm, with a best figure on one leg of MIRA's banked circuit in good conditions of 96 (5,800 rpm). One does not notice much difference in cruising refinement subjectively, though there is obviously some improvement. Fuel consumption overall, compared with the lower-geared car which took part in the Midget-Spitfire double test (*Autocar* 10 April 1969), seems hardly affected. We averaged 29.6 mpg over 1,270 miles with best and worst consumptions of 26 and 35 mpg, depending of course on how one responded to the car's obvious willingness to work hard.

Acceleration is very slightly slower, to a degree only noticed by the ink-recording stopwatch. Showing the double-test car in brackets, from a standing start 50 mph comes up in 9.6sec (9.5), 60 in 14.1 (13.8), the ¼-mile in 19.6 (19.3), and 80 in 29.7 (28.3); the new car will however just achieve 90 mph within the length of MIRA's twin horizontal mile—in 51.3sec—which the other would not. Corresponding figures for the MG 1300 MkII are respectively 9.4sec, 14.1, 19.6, and 28.3, with 90 mph seen at 49.2sec.

Good car in traffic

Such cold comparisons are not to the Midget's advantage, and do less than justice to its likeable character. Coupled with good smooth-road handling and brakes (of which more anon), and good visibility whether or not the hood is down, the performance is more than enough to provide the keen driver with a lot of fun. Clearly what advantages the little MG has are at their best in traffic; one has more than enough go to stay master of most traffic situations. The engine is always willing, beginning to pull hard from 3,000 rpm, though not baulking if you ask it to work from speeds only a little above its tickover. Recommended brief maximum speed is 6,300 rpm on the revcounter, which under-read by 100 rpm at this speed, but the engine feels happy to go higher without signs of valve-bounce. Exhaust and mechanical noise from the engine are not obtrusive; it is the gearbox which offends most clearly here. First gear would not seem out of voice in one of the lower-priced Vintage-period popular cars. It is very noisy on most examples we have tried. Second and 3rd are only somewhat better.

Gear ratios are well-chosen, giving maximum speeds of 33, 55 and 78 mph at 6,400 rpm. Useful maxima for everyday use at 6,000 rpm are 31, 52 and 73 mph. The gearchange is extremely precise, with nothing rubbery about it, and very much in character for the type of car. The Midget shares with its main competitor the Triumph Spitfire the distinction of lacking synchromesh on 1st gear, which omission stands out more clearly as the years roll by. One learns to judge engine and road speeds correctly for double-declutching changes down, but it isn't easy here. On the other hand the renowned flexibility of the A-series engine will enable the lazy or less-skilled driver to use 2nd instead in many instances. The clutch is equally tolerant, coping adequately with the

considerable revs needed to re-start two-up on the 1-in-3 slope.

The Midget's steering is everything a sports-car's ought to be—light, very accurate, highly responsive, highly geared and, once the rack is fully run-in, giving good feel without too much kickback. There is no slop worth mentioning, so that on first driving it, having got out of almost any other car, one tends to "over-steer". The car's obviously rigid construction shows through to the driver on a twisty road; it feels very much all one piece. Slippery roads are fun in the Midget, which is unusually well balanced. Handling characteristics are completely safe; slight initial understeer changing progressively to middling tail-breakaway when you try really hard. There is no suggestion of treachery at any stage, though such a light car obviously badly needs all-independent suspension. Ride is distinctly firm, the live-axled back end hopping outwards somewhat on bumpy bends taken quickly. As usual with an open car one is not conscious of suspension noise to any degree.

Brakes are unassisted discs front, drums

Unlike several other sports-cars, the Midget's hood does not need a lot of practice to furl properly

This view shows how comparatively little three-quarter-rear vision is lost by the large-windowed hood. Rubber-faced overriders are a sensible feature

Neat trim lines still, though you can only buy the car now with the black side-strip paint. There are no nave-plates on the wheels. Right: Wide-angle, lens-distorted view of the Midget in its most pleasant form, with hood down

rear. They work well, giving 1g stopping power on a dry track with the rear wheels just locking at a not-too-heavy 80lb pedal pressure. There is adequate fade resistance for all normal purposes, though anyone using the car at all competitively does well to fit hard pads and linings (available, like much other speed equipment at extra cost, from British Leyland Special Tuning at Abingdon). The handbrake holds the car facing up or down the 1-in-3 slope.

The driving position remains somewhat old-fashioned. Taller drivers have to sit closer to the large steering wheel than they may prefer, and have just enough legroom. The quickness of the steering means that the first objection doesn't matter too much; the second could only be improved by a major redesign of the car. Door openings are rather cramping for getting out, and the too-stiff door releases are much too far back for easy reach. There is however a pleasant feeling of snugness once you're in the very comfortable driving seat. No major control is remote from you, the gearchange falls readily to hand, and the pedals are well arranged.

Heel-and-toe changes come easily, and there is room to rest the left foot on the foot dip-switch. The horn is in the most natural place, the large padded centre of the steering wheel, and makes a surprisingly "quality" noise. Visibility is of course superb with the hood down, except perhaps through the somewhat fussy clutter of the front quarter-lights. It is better-than-average with the hood up, with no serious blind spots.

The facia is pleasingly straightforward, with no ostentatious transatlantic lips and jowls. One would however like to see some extra attention paid to more efficient design—combination of wiper and washer switch and plunger for one thing and, on each door, a more substantial-feeling but less stiff-winding window handle. When it broke away from its fixing screws we learnt that the quite generous parcel shelf on the passenger's side is made of something resembling cardboard. Uprating the crude water-valve may increase the heat output, but it does nothing towards proper control of temperature.

Hood erection and furling is easier than on most British sports-cars. The windscreen-frame clamps need a lot of effort, so does buttoning down the hood-cover press-studs. If one fitted a wireless it would, with the hood up, only be any real use at slow speeds, as wind noise becomes too loud above 60 mph. Keen enthusiasts who prefer to carry out their own servicing will find the Midget's engine accessibility pretty good. They will however need a lot more in tools than comes with the car—in the usual scruffy bag lying loose in the boots of so many British cars. Boot space is limited by the spare wheel, but careful stowage with squashy bags will get quite a lot in.

As stated at the beginning, there is not very much competition for the Midget (and the Sprite). It is a model that fills a large need, and one we would like to see developed considerably without losing its worthy character of sports-car primer for the not-so-well-off younger driver (and slightly dashing shopping car for two-car families). As it is, it remains an excellent little car which certainly achieves its primary object—that of being fun to drive. ☐

ACCELERATION

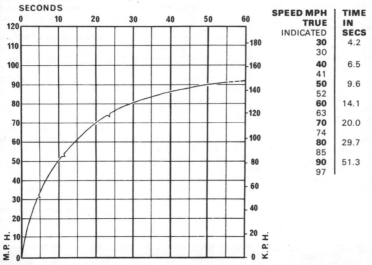

SPEED MPH		TIME
TRUE		IN
INDICATED		SECS
30		4.2
30		
40		6.5
41		
50		9.6
52		
60		14.1
63		
70		20.0
74		
80		29.7
85		
90		51.3
97		

SPEED RANGE, GEAR RATIOS AND TIME IN SECONDS

mph	Top (3.9)	3rd (5.29)	2nd (7.47)	1st (12.48)
10-30	—	8.0	5.5	4.0
20-40	10.7	7.4	5.2	—
30-50	10.4	7.2	6.3	—
40-60	10.7	8.3	—	—
50-70	12.3	10.3	—	—
60-80	16.9	—	—	—
70-90	31.8	—	—	—

Standing ¼-mile
19.6sec 69 mph
Standing kilometre
36.6sec 85mph
Test distance
1,270 miles
Mileage recorder
0.7 per cent
over-reading

PERFORMANCE
MAXIMUM SPEEDS

Gear	mph	kph	rpm
Top (mean)	94	151	5,700
(best)	96	155	5,800
3rd	78	126	6,400
2nd	55	89	6,400
1st	33	53	6,400

BRAKES

(from 70 mph in neutral)
Pedal load for 0.5g stops in lb

1	55-50	6	55-50
2	55-50	7	55-50
3	52-48	8	55-52
4	52-47	9	55-50
5	53-48	10	55-50

RESPONSE (from 30 mph in neutral)

Load	g	Distance
20lb	0.16	188ft
40lb	0.34	89ft
60lb	0.57	53ft
80lb	1.0	30.1ft
Handbrake	0.37	81ft
Max. Gradient 1 in 3		

CLUTCH
Pedal 35lb and 4.5 in.
MOTORWAY CRUISING

Indicated speed at 70mph	74mph
Engine (rpm at 70mph)	4,240rpm
(mean piston speed)	2,260ft/min.
Fuel (mpg at 70mph)	35.7
Passing (50-70mph)	10.4sec

COMPARISONS

MAXIMUM SPEED MPH

MG 1300 Mk II 2-door	(£968)	97
Ford Escort 1300GT 2-door	(£966)	95
MG Midget Mk III	**(£906)**	**94**
Triumph Spitfire 4 Mk 3	(£876)	92
Mini 1275GT	(£894)	86

0-60 MPH, SEC

Ford Escort 1300GT 2-door	12.2
Triumph Spitfire 4 Mk 3	14.0
MG Midget Mk III	**14.1**
MG 1300 Mk II 2-door	14.1
Mini 1275 GT	14.7

STANDING ¼-MILE, SEC

Triumph Spitfire 4 Mk 3	19.4
Ford Escort 1300GT 2-door	19.5
MG Midget Mk III	**19.6**
MG 1300 Mk II 2-door	19.6
Mini 1275 GT	19.8

OVERALL MPG

Triumph Spitfire 4 Mk 3	31.3
Mini 1275GT	30.2
MG Midget Mk III	**29.6**
Ford Escort 1300GT 2-door	27.5
MG 1300 Mk II 2-door	26.8

GEARING (with 145-13in. Michelin ZX tyres)

Top	16.5 mph per 1,000 rpm
3rd	12.15 mph per 1,000 rpm
2nd	8.62 mph per 1,000 rpm
1st	5.16 mph per 1,000 rpm

TEST CONDITIONS:
Weather: Fine. Wind: 5-10 mph. Temperature: 16 deg. C. (60 deg. F). Barometer: 29.7in. hg. Humidity: 40 per cent. Surfaces: Dry concrete and asphalt.

WEIGHT:
Kerb weight 13.8 cwt (1,546lb—702kg) (with oil, water and half full fuel tank). Distribution, per cent F. 52.5; R. 47.5. Laden as tested: 17.3cwt (1,934lb—878kg).

TURNING CIRCLES:
Between kerbs L. 32ft 3in.; R. 32ft 0in. Between walls L. 33ft 7in.; R. 33ft 4in., steering wheel turns, lock to lock 2¼.

Figures taken at 3,200 miles by our own staff at the Motor Industry Research Association proving ground at Nuneaton.

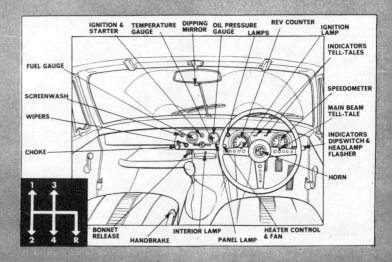

CONSUMPTION

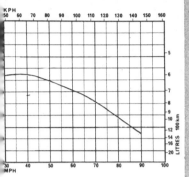

FUEL

at constant speeds—mpg)

) mph	. . . .	47.0
) mph	. . . .	47.6
) mph	. . . .	44.9
) mph	. . . .	40.4
) mph	. . . .	35.7
) mph	. . . .	28.5
) mph	. . . .	22.8

ypical mpg	. . . 30	(9.4 litres/100km)
lculated (DIN) mpg	32.5	(8.7 litres/100km)
verall mpg	. . . 29.6	(9.5 litres/100km)
rade of fuel	Premium, 4-star (min. 97 RM)	

L

iles per pint (SAE 10W/40)	. . . .	1,200

SPECIFICATION FRONT ENGINE, REAR-WHEEL DRIVE

ENGINE

Cylinders	. . .	4, in line
Main bearings	.	3
Cooling system	.	Water; pump, fan and thermostat
Bore	. . . .	70.6mm (2.78 in.)
Stroke	. . . .	81.3mm (3.20 in.)
Displacement	.	1,275 c.c. (77.8 cu. in.)
Valve gear	. . .	Overhead; pushrods and rockers
Compression ratio	8.8-to-1 Min. octane rating: 97 RM	
Carburettors	. .	Twin SU HS2
Fuel pump	. . .	SU electric
Oil filter	. . . .	Full-flow, renewable element
Max. power	. .	64 bhp (net) at 5,800 rpm
Max. torque	.	72 lb.ft (net) at 3,000 rpm

TRANSMISSION

Clutch	. . . .	Borg and Beck diaphragm spring 6.5in. dia.
Gearbox	. . . .	Four speed, synchromesh on 2nd, 3rd and top
Gear ratios	. . .	Top 1.0
		Third 1.357
		Second 1.916
		First 3.2
		Reverse 4.14
Final drive	. . .	Hypoid bevel 3.90-to-1

CHASSIS and BODY

Construction	. .	Integral, with steel body

SUSPENSION

Front	. . . . .	Independent, coil springs, wishbones, lever-arm dampers, optional anti-roll bar (not fitted to test car)
Rear	. . . . .	Live axle, half-elliptic leaf springs, lever arm dampers

STEERING

Type	. . . . .	Rack and pinion
Wheel dia.	. . .	16in.

BRAKES

Make and type	.	Lockheed discs front, drums rear, no servo
Dimensions	. .	F 8.25in. dia
		R 7in. dia 1.25in. wide shoes.
Swept area	. .	F 135 sq. in., R 55 sq. in.
		Total 190 sq. in. (220 sq. in./ton laden)

WHEELS

Type	. . . . .	Pressed steel perforated disc, four-stud fixing (wire wheels optional) 4.0 in. wide rim.
Tyres—make	. .	(cross-ply standard) Michelin on test car.
—type	. .	ZX radial ply tubeless.
—size	. .	145-13 in.

EQUIPMENT

Battery	. . . .	12 Volt 43 Ah
Generator	. . .	Lucas C40 28 amp d.c.
Headlamps	. . .	Sealed beam, 120/90 watt (total)
Reversing lamp	.	Standard
Electric fuses	. .	4
Screen wipers	.	Single speed, self-parking
Screen washer	.	Standard, manual plunger
Interior heater	.	Standard, water-valve
Heated backlight	.	Not applicable
Safety belts	. .	Extra, anchorages built in
Interior trim	. .	Pvc seats, pvc headlining
Floor covering	.	Carpet
Jack	. . . . .	Screw pillar
Jacking points	.	One each side in centre of body
Windscreen	. .	Toughened
Underbody protection	.	Phosphate treatment under paint

MAINTENANCE

Fuel tank	. . .	6 Imp. gallons (no reserve) (27.3 litres)
Cooling system	.	6 pints (including heater)
Engine sump	. .	6.5 pints (3.7 litres) SAE 10W/40. Change oil every 6,000 miles. Change filter element every 6,000 miles.
Gearbox	. . . .	2.5 pints SAE 10W/40. Top up every 12,000 miles.
Final drive	. . .	1.5 pints SAE 90EP. Top up every 12,000 miles
Grease	. . . .	7 points every 3,000 miles
Tyre pressures	. .	F 22; R 24 psi (normal driving) F26, R 28 psi (fast driving) F 22; R 26 psi (full load)
Max. payload	. .	350 lb (159 kg.)

PERFORMANCE DATA

Top gear mph per 1,000 rpm	. . . .	16.5
Mean piston speed at max. power	. .	3,200 ft/min.
Bhp per ton laden	. . . .	74

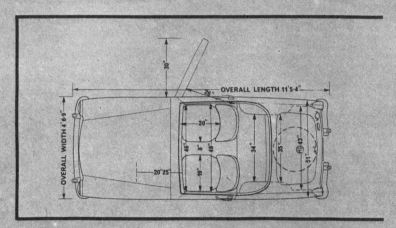

STANDARD GARAGE 16ft x 8ft 6in.

OVERALL LENGTH 11'5·4"

OVERALL WIDTH 4'6·9"

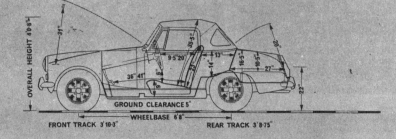

SCALE 0.3in. to 1ft
Cushions uncompressed

OVERALL HEIGHT 4'0·6"

GROUND CLEARANCE 5"
WHEELBASE 6'8"
FRONT TRACK 3'10·3"
REAR TRACK 3'8·75"

Dr Stokes' Monkey-Gland Machines

Can the endless rehashes
subdue the wrinkles on BL's Midget and
Spitfire for much longer? Our
Giant Test team gives
its mini report . . .

PERFORMANCE	
MG Midget	Triumph Spitfire
0–30 3.9	0–30 4.4 seconds
40 5.9	40 6.4
50 9.5	50 10.5
60 13.8	60 15
70 19.0	70 23.8
80 28.2	80 34.1

MAXIMUM SPEED

96mph	91mph

FUEL CONSUMPTION

27mpg	28mpg

FOR

Higher performance	Reasonable performance
Lower price	Good handling
Smaller dimensions	Better roadholding
	Lower noise levels
	Roomier cockpit

AGAINST

Cramped driving position	Poor ride
Poor ride	
Indifferent roadholding	

▶YOUNG ENTHUSIASTS— not to mention a few other categories of driver—have been choosing between MG Midget and Triumph Spitfire for quite a while now. Having decided to ignore small GT saloons and go the sports car route there's precious little else to consider. Kit cars are ruled out for the majority by inferior marketing, lack of service facilities and guarantees as much as anything else—a lot more people would buy Ginettas and the like if they knew more about them because they are very good. So it comes back to what the big manufacturers have to offer—and that's not much. The British-based American trio are content, as are most Continentals, to leave this specialised field to British Leyland.

Even if there were challengers they would find BL's pair pretty well entrenched. The Midget, now priced at £970, in its present basic form has been around for 10 years and its ancestry stretches back to 1958 when the Austin Healey Sprite, from which it is derived, came on the scene. The Midget is no more than a Sprite by another badge but now that the Healey name for trade use is reverting to Donald of that ilk (and will next be seen on a Jensen-built sports car) the Sprite part of the duo is due to disappear ere long.

The cousin/rival Triumph, £55 dearer, isn't that much younger. But, like the Midget, it's received enough modifications and improvements over the years to maintain much of its original appeal. On the Spitfire the latest batch of changes concerned the appearance and (belatedly) the suspension.

Let's deal with the looks first. The big change was around the tail, where the fussy, rounded rump was sliced off to be replaced by a cleaner, notched transom copied from big brother Stag. At the front the ugly raised seams along the wing tops were removed. The panel joint was moved down to the side of the wing and is now made by folding the sheet metal inwards rather than out. The top of the wing was re-finished with a razor-edge. At the same time the headlamps got painted instead of chrome bezels and the nose treatment was tidied up in detail. The overall result is a cleaner, altogether more pleasing shape that has lost all the cheapness imparted by the chrome-tipped wings of earlier models. It's a pity the budget didn't run to similar

treatment for the rear wings. They still have the shiny strip but at least it's not so noticeable there.

The Midget changed rather less at its last facelift. It got some black paint along the rocker panels in a partially successful attempt to make the lines less dumpy. Some chunky-patterned steel wheels became standard, with wires an option as on the Spitfire, and the bonnet and boot were equipped with self-propping stays.

Black paint or no, the Midget is a full foot shorter than the better-proportioned Spitfire. And it looks it from most angles.

On getting in you will probably conclude that all 12 inches have been saved in the cockpit. The cramped quarters of the Midget come as an instant reminder of its aged basic design. Back then, it seems, a significant number of people thought it all right to be cramped into a sports car, arms akimbo and legs splayed. Today they don't with the result that the cockpit is best suited to midgets or sub-teenage children. Unfortunately the cockpit room has stayed unchanged over the years but the seats have become thicker and plusher. Since kids are unlikely to be driving it and midgets are in short supply (that was unintentional, I promise) the cockpit poses a problem for the rest of us. Even with the very limited seat travel used up the largish wheel is still stuck in your chest and you're sitting bow-legged at the pedals. Facia and windscreen are disconcertingly close, and so is everything else in the cockpit.

The Spitfire seems almost roomy by comparison. Six-footers can get far enough away from wheel and pedals for comfort and to drivers of all shapes and sizes the higher seating position means better visibility than in the Midget.

In both cars there's a space behind the seats that comes in handy for tucking away small objects. Or it does when the hood is erect. Furled, the soft top hogs most of this compartment.

The hoods currently in use have come a long way from those of the earliest Midgets and Spitfires. They can be folded down in proper convertible style, the frames remaining attached to the body. On the Spitfire plastic covers are used on the rails passing near the occupants' heads. In both instances raising or lowering the top is several minutes' work, best done by two people although one can cope quite well alone. As ever, the windscreen rail clamps have a

tensioning function and need more muscle than many a woman can muster even in a crisis like rain. Even the frailest woman, however, should have little trouble with the rest of the controls. The Triumph's are particularly light to use, though some might want a servo or at least more progressive action on the rather dead brake pedal, while the Midget's gearchange was stiffer than it should have been. Experience shows that these boxes improve with age...

The customary sports car instrumentation of speedo and tacho, fuel level, oil pressure and water temperature gauges occurs on the Midget. The Spitfire relies on a warning light for oil pressure. We thought the layout of the instruments, also the minor controls and switches, ill-considered —in fact, confusing—on both.

This is all the more a pity when you remember that sports machines like these are supposedly *the* cars for enthusiastic drivers. But enthusiasts, according to the gospel of British Leyland, don't mind that sort of thing. Neither, apparently, are they supposed to mind the inefficient heating and ventilation systems of this pair. The Midget has opening quarterlights, the Spitfire not, but both had gaps between hood and windscreen or window through which fresh air could enter. Neither car has proper direction-controllable fresh air outlets. And the heating controls function with all the precision and predictability of an ageing geyser.

There are other things too that you have to put up with in these 1971 sports cars. Wind roar plus mechanical noise (and the usual terrible transmission whine in the Midget) and suitably burpy exhausts combine to make a din that precludes conversation above 60mph. Even at a meagre 40 or so the Spitfire is becoming a trifle wearing and the Midget is already downright noisy.

Equally tiresome is the ride on anything but a billiards table of a surface. Bumps, especially the kind that abound on country lanes, soon have the Spitfire joggling like a massage machine. The harder sprung Midget feels the bumps even more. So do its occupants.

These high noise levels and rotten ride qualities were once supposed to be part of the fun— an inescapable part of high performance motoring. Well, Chapman proved years ago with the Lotus that suspension doesn't have to be hard to work correctly.

Saloon designers have found ways of sound damping that would apply to the Triumph and MG. And in any case the performance is not all that high for 1971!

The days when sports cars were automatically the masters of the saloon are over. We would back a comparable GT saloon, say Ford's 1300 GT Escort or the 1275 GT Mini, to match the Spitfire and Midget lap for lap on a racing circuit. The saloons have been catching up in both handling and performance over the last few years and some of them are now level-pegging if not ahead of the alleged sports cars.

Until last autumn, in fact, we would have doubted the Spitfire's ability even to equal some of its more staid rivals when it came to cornering. Up to that date, you will recall, its Herald parentage meant that it was cursed with the same swing-axle rear end. This meant that initial understeer switched abruptly and prematurely to oversteer as the high rear roll centre jacked the back up and let the wheels droop in a classic positive-camber knock-kneed pose. The effect could be induced even earlier and for the novice even more unsettlingly by driving into a corner and then lifting off.

Eventually, rather late in the day, Triumph put a stop to this. The current Mk IV Spitfire has not the wishbone-geometry rear end of the once similarly afflicted GT6 but an ingenious modification of existing components. Only the master leaf of the transverse rear spring is clamped to the chassis. The rest of the leaves are held via a rubber pad on to a pivot so that they still support the car's weight but can also rock about their axis. Thus practically all roll stiffness has been eliminated from the rear end. At the front it has been increased by a corresponding amount with a thicker anti-roll bar. So the Spitfire rolls no more than before, which is to say very little, but with nearly all the roll loading on the outer front tyre it is now a reformed character. It still starts out with understeer but that changes to near neutral handling as the *g* force increases and only changes to oversteer at an advanced stage and then in a highly controllable fashion. So the Spitfire has gained in both handling, for it can now be thrown around with abandon *and* confidence, and roadholding, inasmuch as that sheer cornering power is now a good deal higher than before. All this still with the basic swing axle...

Such developments put it rather a long way ahead of the poor old Midget. Hampered by its leaf-sprung back axle, harder suspension settings as well as stiff damping, plus an inordinately short (6ft 8in) wheelbase the MG remains very much a leaper from crag to crag. Bumps easily unsettle a sometimes tenuous grip on the road, making it hard to tell when axle hop ends and unadulterated oversteer begins. The cramped driving position does little to encourage dashing tactics.

Like the Spitfire, the Midget has a disappointingly dead-feeling disc front/drum rear brake system.

Being based largely on bits and pieces from saloons this pair have extremely familiar engines. The A series unit in the Midget and the Spitfire's ex-Standard engine share the usual basic features: three main bearings, for instance, and pushrod valves, not to mention constricted porting and other things that impede development. Notwithstanding this, Triumph manage to get a respectable 63bhp out of the 1296cc capacity, with the knowledge that there's more to come just from changing to the long-stroke crank used in the 1500 saloon. But there could be a problem here with bearings.

Journal sizes went up less than a year ago in an attempt to increase bearing life; higher loadings from enlarged capacity could put the engineers back to square one.

The Midget's aged but still willing A series is fractionally more efficient, producing one extra bhp from 21 fewer ccs. For some reason we have yet to fathom BLMC is keeping some power up its corporate sleeve here for the similarly-engined MG 1300 gets an extra six bhp which wouldn't come amiss in the two-seater. Nor would it mean any loss in flexibility for the Midget is more than sufficiently amenable to lugging along in too high a gear if a lazy driver insists. The Spitfire is not so happy under these conditions, losing out not so much on tractability of the power unit as in the snatch that overrun all too easily builds up in the multi-jointed transmission.

Talking of transmission, though, the Spitfire does score easily in the cog-changing part of the drive line. For a start, it now actually has synchromesh on bottom gear (where *will* all this development end, one wonders) while the Midget continues to lack this feature—almost alone among 1971 cars. Just to compound the felony, first is none too easy to

engage on the move, and sometimes at rest, even with competent double-declutching. The Spitfire scores again by making overdrive available as an extra-cost option. It works on third and top and is controlled by a switch built into the gear knob. Very convenient.

The presence of overdrive does a lot for fuel consumption (in addition to enhancing general drivability) which in our hard-driving hands averaged around 28mpg, though many an owner is probably getting better than 30. Another factor here was the recent step up in axle ratio from 4.11 to 3.89 to one. The other side of this coin is of course that the higher final drive knocks something off the acceleration. In this case the Spitfire certainly felt a little less lively than earlier models and confirmed our fears by its acceleration figures.

The Midget, gaining from its much lower weight, proved quicker by a useful amount all the way up to maximum. Initial acceleration would have been even better were it not for a recent increase in the ratio of that accursed first gear. Fuel consumption at 27mpg was only slightly heavier.

Neither car stood out as a sparkling performer in ultimate terms. There are plenty of 1300s around that can match their acceleration and top speed. The difference is that these other 1300s are saloons, with four seats.

So why buy a little two-seater unless you're a masochist? Well, there's no doubt that they're fun to drive. Sitting down there with that long bonnet out front, amidst all the mechanical clamour, you feel part of the action in a way you never can in a saloon. Then there's that huge 20th century myth about sports cars that has permeated the whole Western world: they do things for a young man's style, and make implications about his virility that no small saloon can match. Which, you might sardonically point out, is why they sell so well in America where extroverts are thicker on the ground. They're an incitement to quick motoring. They make every journey feel an epic of automotive adventure.

The Midget feels outdated now though the much more modern Spitfire should be good for a few more years yet—especially with the boost of a 1500 engine. But manufacturing costs are soaring for these relatively limited output cars and are being forced up even higher as the parental saloons are discontinued as times change. ●

The engines of the Midget (top) and Spitfire are old faithfuls, the 1275cc MG unit dating back to Morris Minors of the 1950s. Strangely, in MG form it gives less power than in the Cooper S. The Spitfire unit is shared with the Herald and in updated form with the Toledo, and also dates from way back in the days when Standard made cars

The Spitfire interior (top) is more simple and functional than that of the MG, with better leg room and a more satisfactory facia. The Spitfire's hood can be unclipped and folded fairly quickly but the MG's takes longer

MIDGET MODS

Some driving impressions of the latest MG Midget Mk. III

Generally neat and functional if not outstandingly pretty, the latest Midget's appearance is improved by the rounded rear wheel arches. Its Mk I Sprite ancestry is still evident from the curved bonnet-to-side member join line behind the front wheel arch

Some small changes made to the highly successful MG Midget last January gave us an opportunity to once again sample this old-fashioned but still very enjoyable small sports car. They also marked the final farewell to production of the mechanically identical Austin-Healey Sprite, whose frog-eyed quarter-elliptic rear sprung ancestor began a minor success story for what has become British Leyland.

THE obvious recognition points for the car spotter are the Rostyle wheels—a big improvement on the very bogus-looking affairs previously fitted in our opinion—and the enlarged, round-eyelidded rear wheel arches, also we think much nicer than the previous flat-topped ones. Most useful of the unseen changes is the adoption of a 16½ per cent larger capacity for the petrol tank, now a nominal 7 gallons instead of only 6. Inside the cockpit there are now improved quality carpets, softer 'safety' door pulls, a larger gearlever knob—a small but very

welcome change on any sporting car—and rocker switches instead of toggles.

It is still noticeable how much of the highly individual character of the old Mk 1 Sprite there is about even this latest Midget. Certainly the very amusing but not very high-grip tail-happiness of the original car disappeared long ago with those quarter ellipties, but the same snug 'right' feeling is still there. Particularly if you have been spoilt by the not inconsiderable number of motor cars around which go faster, you tend to get into the Midget ready to be disappointed.

And certainly its performance is not startling. There isn't any syncromesh on first gear, not on the one we drove anyway. The ride is pure sports car, and the tight little cockpit though roomy enough for even a six-footer imposes a close-to-the-wheel driving position that will take some people right back to its namesake of 40 years ago.

But—and the 'but' is a good one—there is something about the little beast. Its steering is most marvellously quick by modern standards, also completely accurate in the way that only a good rack and

AOH 619K

MIDGET
MODS...

pinion set up can be. The gearchange is a delight, and one enjoys getting a proper change into first right again. Its size makes it simplicity itself to poke through gaps, remembering always that the same factor dictates more than usual care on the part of the driver for fear he may not be seen. And although the stiff springing makes it hop about somewhat on bumpy country bends, it never hops too far, and the roadholding on Michelin X's is very

good. So much so in fact that one has to restrain oneself from having a go at all sorts of other people through a series of corners, Minis included.

One joy of even the simplest sports cars is that usually (though not always) one is very comfortably placed, whether driver or passenger. The Midget is no exception, because the driver soon gets used to the old-fashioned driving position, and certainly feels one with the car. The seats hold one quite well. Heel-and-toe work with the pedals is easy, unlike the arrangement on the Midget's big brother the MGB which always to my amazement needs some work on the throttle pedal before it can be driven properly. With the hood up visibility is not bad, but as usual the car comes into its own with the hood down. Getting the top down is still not

nearly as simple as it ought to be—we wish someone at British Leyland would take a long careful look at the incredibly simple arrangement on the Alfa Romeo 1750 Spider Veloce—you can if you feel like it put that up or take it down whilst driving gently.

It is fortunate for British Leyland that no one has ever seriously attempted to challenge their position in the admittedly limited small sports-car market; both the Midget and its less successful rival from Triumph would do well with a combined re-think. That does not alter the fact that the Midget is still the right way for the young man who is keen on driving to start (assuming he can find a tolerant insurance company). The reason is that this little MG is true fun, which is what a sports car is for in any language. **Michael Scarlett**

Rocker switches and a better carpet are the principal changes visible here inside; the driving position is very snug, suiting the relatively high-geared steering. Under the bonnet there are no immediately obvious modifications; accessibility is good. The boot allows just enough room for a weekend's squashy luggage for two

by John Bolster

Midget takes a lot of beating

The small, open, sports two-seater was invented by the French in the nineteen-twenties. In earlier times, sports cars were apt to be huge, chain-driven, and German, but the French, having organised many races for *Voiturettes* produced a marvellous range of racy little sports *bolides*, Bugattis, Salmsons, Amilcars, Senechals, Rallys, BNCs, Lombards, Ratiers—but I could go on for the rest of the page.

It is history that Britain took over the sports car market and in the nineteen-thirties an open sports car usually carried a GB plate, while large numbers of them also exhibited an octagon badge, containing the magic letters, MG. After the war, the Americans belatedly discovered the sports car and the MG became a mighty dollar earner. Since then, the USA has adopted a plethora of 'safety' regulations, most of which make a car more dangerous by spoiling its handling and reducing its acceleration.

To build a sports car that will fulfil all these crazy requirements is difficult indeed and MG are to be congratulated on getting through the labyrinth, while other sports car manufacturers have given up in despair. Unfortunately, the cars for the USA and UK markets come off the same production lines, and so we must buy our Midgets weighed down with huge American bumpers, or go without.

This is a pity, but nothing can compare with a real open car on a summer's day, and the Midget is still an attractive little machine. Though its weight has gone up, it now has a 1493cc Triumph engine instead of the 1275cc A-series unit, which enables it to out-perform such modern competitors as the Fiat X1/9. In the vintage era, the MG would have been called a drophead coupé, because it has winding windows and a folding hood. Though it is appreciably faster with the top up, it is as an *open* sports car that it really appeals.

In open form, the Midget is surprisingly quiet and not at all draughty. There's some luggage space in the boot and a lot more behind the seats, so this is an ideal holiday car for two. When parking, one can quickly button on the cockpit cover, in case of rain. In passing, may I ask manufacturers if they will please, please not refer to this useful accessory as a tonneau cover? The tonneau is the rear half of an open four-seater, so you can't have a tonneau cover on a two-seater car!

In closed form, the MG is completely weather-proof and very cosy, a useful small town car,

in fact. It is also extremely noisy at high speeds, most of the general hubbub being generated by the wind passing over the fabric. It is possible to make a quiet hood, but it needs careful profiling and support in exactly the right places. The hood of the MG has evidently not been developed in the wind tunnel, and it shows. This is a splendid hood for moderate speeds around town, but it simply isn't acceptable for a long, fast trip.

I found the MG very easy to enter, though it is perhaps a little difficult for portly persons to place their posteriors; I judged the driving position comfortable and a shorter driver was equally at home. The gearchange is rapid and simple, all the controls being well-placed, and though the younger generation might like a smaller wheel, set rather further away, I would not quarrel with the present arrangement. The engine starts instantly, hot or cold, and only becomes noisy when pressed towards its limit. However, there's plenty of torque if one changes up a little earlier than that.

The steering is quite high-geared and pleasantly light to handle, but the car needs more holding to a straight course than is usual nowadays. On corners it tends to oversteer, especially on lift-off, which calls for rapid correction. Some drivers enjoy handling a car that is set up in this way, and it's fun to apply bags of opposite lock. On the other hand, oversteer is a condition of instability, and some modern drivers, who have never met it before, might be caught out. I believe that this characteristic stems from a raised suspension height, which is part of the American package, but certainly the fabulous controllability of earlier Midgets seems to have been lost to some extent. The brakes are well up to their work and smooth in action.

The latest Midget has a good performance—it's a genuine 100mph car—and as an open car for enjoying the fresh air it takes a lot of beating; detachable "Targa" tops or sliding sunshine roofs are poor substitutes. Many sports car drivers prefer a hard ride, and they will appreciate this machine, but I would ask for more suspension travel, and there are parts of France and Spain where the MG would be almost unbearable if driven at all fast. However, for the better roads of England it does quite well and I enjoyed driving it enormously in the beautiful summer sunshine; it looked the part in its brilliant yellow paint job, too.

Above: our Technical Editor aboard the MG Midget—it still takes a lot of beating if you appreciate fresh air. An enormously enjoyable little car.

Specification and performance data

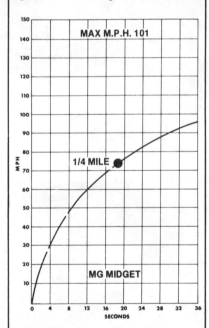

Car tested: MG Midget sports 2-seater, price £2,647.
Engine: Four cylinders 73.7 × 87.5mm (1493cc). Compression ratio 9 to 1. 66bhp DIN at 5500rpm. Pushrod-operated overhead valves. Twin SU carburetters.
Transmission: Single dry plate clutch. 4-speed synchromesh gearbox, ratios: 1.0, 1.43, 2.11, and 3.41 to 1. Hypoid rear axle, ratio 3.9 to 1.
Chassis: Integral steel construction. Independent front suspension by wishbones and coil springs with anti-roll bar. Rack and pinion steering. Live rear axle on semi-elliptic springs. Disc/drum brakes. Bolt-on steel wheels, fitted 145-13 tyres.
Equipment: 12-volt lighting and starting. Speedometer. Rev-counter. Water temperature, oil-pressure, and fuel gauges. Heating and demisting. Windscreen wipers and washers. Reversing lights.
Dimensions: Wheelbase 6ft 8in, track 3ft 10.3in/3ft 8.75in. Overall length 11ft 9in. Width 5ft 0.25in. Weight 15.4cwt.
Performance: Maximum speed 101mph. Speeds in gears: third 70mph, second 47mph, first 28mph. Standing quarter-mile 18.4s. Acceleration: 0-30mph 3.9s, 0-50mph 8.6s, 0-60mph 12.2s, 0-80mph 23.8s.
Fuel consumption: 28 to 34mpg.

AUTO TEST

MG Midget 1500

1,493 c.c.

Smallest British Leyland sports car given much more punch by bigger engine. Quick, accurate steering but handling throttle-sensitive and inclined to oversteer. Harsh ride, excessive wind noise with hood up. Undergeared. Limited range

The Midget rolls considerably when cornered hard and the outside front wheel becomes heavily loaded as seen here. If at this point the steering wheel is held steady the car increasingly oversteers as the corner continues; lifting off the accelerator causes the tail to twitch sharply outwards

THERE was an outburst of lamentation from MG enthusiasts when the Midget 1500 was announced, apparently because the A-series engine had been replaced by a Triumph-designed unit. From an engineering point of view the change was almost inevitable. The Midget needed a bigger engine to counteract the effect of safety and antipollution equipment in America, where it sells in its greatest numbers; and at 1,275 c.c., the A-series unit was at the end of its "stretch potential". The answer was to instal the Triumph engine which, while of similar design and vintage, had long ago been given a longer stroke to bring its capacity to 1,493 c.c., its first application being the now-defunct front-drive Triumph 1500.

The purists may decry the move, but Triumph is a name long respected in the sports car business and there is no reason to suppose the Spitfire engine should be unsuitable for the Midget. It might be more in order to complain that a considerable increase in swept volume has resulted in a negligible increase in quoted power, from 64 bhp (net) to 66 bhp (DIN). On the other hand torque, a more important part of a sports car's character than most people realize, is increased by a greater margin. Against all this has to be balanced the greater weight of the new car, with a kerb weight (our measurement) of 15·3cwt compared with the 13·8cwt of the last 1,275 c.c. Midget we tested.

Performance and economy

The proof of the Midget 1500 is in the stopwatch, and there is no doubt it is substantially quicker than the late-series 1,275 c.c. car. Comparisons are valid because the final drive ratio remains unchanged at 3·9 to 1; the adoption of the single-rail "corporate" gearbox has meant some change in internal ratios, which are wider than before. Tyre size likewise remains the same.

The Midget 1500 is a genuine 100 mph car, and this represents a great advance on the 1275 which managed only 94 mph mean when tested in 1971. Unfortunately maximum speed takes the car over the red line on its rev counter, which over-read by a modest 100 rpm at maximum speed; clearly, therefore the Midget is substantially undergeared to make best use of its peak power, which falls at 5,500 rpm. Higher gearing would not only improve economy, but also permit higher speeds in the intermediate gears.

Although we ran the Midget beyond the 6,000 rpm red line to attain its ultimate maximum speed, we stuck to the limit in the lower gears with the result that first gear would not quite take the car to 30 mph, and third stopped just short of 70 mph. Our figures point up the considerable gap between second (47 mph maximum) and third, which is felt on the road to some extent but is disguised by the spread of useful torque.

Open sports cars always suffer in performance at the top end when they are run with the hood down, and the Midget was no exception. Lowering the hood took the maximum speed down to 94 mph – apart from making life very uncomfortable at that speed. We took no acceleration figures with the hood down, but there is no doubt they would be inferior to those obtained with the hood in place.

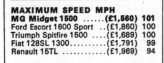
MG Midget 1500

All the Midget 1500 acceleration figures are far superior to those of the 1275, whether from a standing start or in any particular gear. Standing starts are best accomplished without a surfeit of revs and sudden engagement of the clutch, which tends to produce strong and uncomfortable axle tramp. A more gentle procedure, feeding in the clutch fairly fast from a 2,000 rpm starting point, trims half a second off the 1275 time to 30 mph, giving a respectable 3·7sec to this speed. The 1500 proceeds to 60 mph in 12·3sec (a 1·8sec improvement), and to 90 mph in 35·3sec, a better time by no less than 16sec. In like fashion, the standing quarter-mile now takes 18·5sec compared with 19·6 before.

In the gears, every single feature claimed by the 1275 is bettered by a substantial margin. Not only is the torque curve flatter; the 1500 does not run out of breath so quickly at the top end, while flexibility is improved to the extent of being able to pull away from 10 mph in top, which the 1275 would not tolerate.

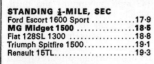

Comparisons

MAXIMUM SPEED MPH

MG Midget 1500	(£1,560)	101
Ford Escort 1600 Sport	(£1,860)	100
Triumph Spitfire 1500	(£1,689)	100
Fiat 128SL 1300	(£1,791)	99
Renault 15TL	(£1,969)	94

0–60 MPH, SEC

Ford Escort 1600 Sport	10·3
MG Midget 1500	12·3
Fiat 128SL 1300	13·1
Triumph Spitfire 1500	13·2
Renault 15TL	13·6

STANDING ¼-MILE, SEC

Ford Escort 1600 Sport	17·9
MG Midget 1500	18·5
Fiat 128SL 1300	18·8
Triumph Spitfire 1500	19·1
Renault 15TL	19·3

OVERALL MPG

Renault 15TL	31·8
Triumph Spitfire 1500	29·1
Fiat 128SL 1300	28·5
MG Midget 1500	27·9
Ford Escort 1600 Sport	27·5

Performance

ACCELERATION SECONDS

True speed mph	Time in Secs	Car Speedo mph
30	3·7	30
40	5·8	40
50	8·5	50
60	12·3	61
70	17·0	71
80	24·0	82
90	35·3	92
100	—	102

Standing ¼-mile
18·5sec 72 mph

Standing kilometre
34·9sec 90 mph

Mileage recorder: accurate

GEAR RATIOS AND TIME IN SEC

mph	Top (3·90)	3rd (5·58)	2nd (8·23)
10–30	9·8	6·2	3·9
20–40	9·2	5·8	4·0
30–50	8·7	5·8	—
40–60	9·6	6·7	—
50–70	10·2	7·9	—
60–80	12·5	—	—
70–90	19·3	—	—

GEARING (with 145–13in. tyres)

Top	16·44 mph per 1,000 rpm
3rd	11·50 mph per 1,000 rpm
2nd	7·79 mph per 1,000 rpm
1st	4·82 mph per 1,000 rpm

MAXIMUM SPEEDS

Gear	mph	khp	rpm
Top (mean)	101	163	6,140*
(best)	102	164	6,200*
3rd	69	111	6,000
2nd	47	76	6,000
1st	29	47	6,000

*See text

BRAKES

FADE (from 70 mph in neutral)
Pedal load for 0·5g stops in lb

1	35	6	45–65
2	40–45	7	50–65
3	40–60	8	50–65
4	45–65	9	50–65
5	45–55	10	50–60

RESPONSE (from 30 mph in neutral)

Load	g	Distance
20lb	0·22	137ft
40lb	0·46	65ft
60lb	0·70	43ft
80lb	0·96	31ft
Handbrake	0·33	91ft
Max Gradient	1 in 3	

CLUTCH
Pedal 42lb and 4¾in.

Consumption

FUEL
(At constant speed – mpg)

30 mph	48·8
40 mph	44·5
50 mph	39·2
60 mph	34·2
70 mph	29·8
80 mph	26·2
90 mph	22·1
100 mph	17·6

Typical mpg 30 (9·4 litres/100km)
Calculated (DIN) mpg 32·5 (8·7 litres/100km)
Overall mpg 27·9 (10·1 litres/100km)
Grade of fuel Premium, 4-star (min 97RM)

OIL
Consumption (SAE 20W/50) 1,000 mpp

TEST CONDITIONS:
Weather: Fine
Wind: 0·3 mph
Temperature: 15deg C (58deg F)
Barometer: 29·95in. Hg
Humidity: 65 per cent
Surface: Dry concrete and asphalt
Test distance 883 miles

Figures taken by our own staff at the Motor Industry Research Association proving ground at Nuneaton.

Dimensions

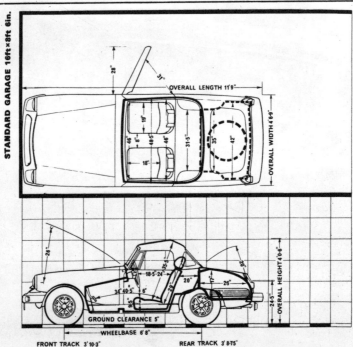

STANDARD GARAGE 16ft × 8ft 6in.

OVERALL LENGTH 11'9"

OVERALL WIDTH 4'6·9"

OVERALL HEIGHT 4'0·6"

GROUND CLEARANCE 5"

WHEELBASE 6'8"

FRONT TRACK 3'10·3"   REAR TRACK 3'8·75"

TURNING CIRCLES:
Between kerbs
L, 30ft 10in.; R, 31ft 11in.
Between walls
L, 32ft 2in.; R, 33ft 3in.
Steering wheel turns, lock to lock 2¾

WEIGHT:
Kerb Weight 15·4cwt
(1,720lb–780kg)
(with oil, water and half full fuel tank)
Distribution, per cent
F, 53·7; R, 46·3
Laden as tested:
18·0cwt (2,020lb–917kg)

Where economy is concerned, one might expect the 1500 to be less economical because of its larger engine. On the other hand its economy should at least be comparable, because the car remains the same size and there is no reason why any more power should be needed to push it along. Two factors upset this tidy calculation. One is that the Midget in its new form is a good deal heavier; the other is its extra performance, which is used some if not all of the time. As a result, our overall fuel consumption emerged as 27·9 mpg compared with 29·6 mpg for the smaller-engined car. This is not a particularly good figure – worse than the Spitfire 1500 for instance, but then the Spitfire has higher gearing and, for our test, overdrive as well. It was noticeable, though, that the Midget's consumption stayed almost constant whoever the driver and whatever the journey, and at no time did it record a brim-to-brim figure of better than 30 mpg.

This is not to say that 30 mpg is unattainable. Our steady-speed figures show that cruising at a constant 60 mph (with the hood up!) enables the driver to better that figure with ease. If this limit were observed and fierce acceleration avoided, the Midget would prove quite economical; but it is not inherently so, still less the way it is likely to be driven.

Handling and brakes
The Midget sticks to its simple suspension arrangement with double wishbones at the front

---

Specification   MG Midget 1500

FRONT ENGINE, REAR-WHEEL DRIVE

ENGINE
Cylinders	4, in line
Main bearings	3
Cooling system	Water; pump, fan and thermostat
Bore	73·7mm (2·90in.)
Stroke	87·5mm (3·44in.)
Displacement	1,493 c.c. (91·1 cu. in.)
Valve gear	Overhead : pushrods and rockers
Compression ratio	9·0 to 1. Min octane rating : 97RM
Carburettors	2 SU HS4
Fuel pump	SU mechanical
Oil filter	Full-flow, replaceable cartridge
Max power	66 bhp (DIN) at 5,500 rpm
Max torque	77 lb. ft. (DIN) at 3,000 rpm

TRANSMISSION
Clutch	Diaphragm-spring, 7·25in. diameter
Gearbox	4-speed, all-synchromesh
Gear ratios	Top 1·0
	Third 1·43
	Second 2·11
	First 3·41
	Reverse 3·75

Final drive	Hypoid bevel, ratio 3·90 to 1
Mph at 1,000 rpm in top gear	16·44

CHASSIS AND BODY
Construction	Integral, with steel body

SUSPENSION
Front	Independent : double wishbones, lever arm dampers, anti-roll bar
Rear	Live axle, semi-elliptic leaf springs, lever-arm dampers

STEERING
Type	Rack and pinion
Wheel dia	15½in.

BRAKES
Type	Disc front, drum rear
Dimensions	F 8·25in. dia R, 7·0in. dia, 1·25in. wide shoes
Swept area	F, 135 sq. in., R, 55 sq. in. Total 190 sq. in. (211 sq. in./ton laden)

WHEELS
Type	Pressed steel Rostyle, 4-stud fixing, 4in. wide rim
Tyres – make	Pirelli Cinturato (on test car)
– type	Radial ply tubeless
– size	145–13in.

EQUIPMENT
Battery	12 volt 40 Ah.
Alternator	28 amp a.c.
Headlamps	Sealed beam, 120/90 watt (total)
Reversing lamp	Standard
Electric fuses	4
Screen wipers	Single-speed
Screen washer	Standard, manual plunger
Interior heater	Standard, water valve type
Heated backlight	Not available
Safety belts	Static type
Interior trim	Pvc seats
Floor covering	Carpet
Jack	Screw pillar type
Jacking points	One each side
Windscreen	Toughened
Underbody protection	Phosphate treatment under paint

MAINTENANCE
Fuel tank	7 Imp gallons (32 litres)
Cooling system	7½ pints (inc heater)
Engine sump	8 pints (4·5 litres) SAE 20W–50. Change oil every 6,000 miles. Change filter every 6,000 miles
Gearbox	1·5 pints. SAE 90EP. Check every 6,000 miles
Final drive	1·75 pints. SAE 90EP. Check every 6,000 miles
Grease	8 points every 6,000 miles
Valve clearance	Inlet 0·010in. (cold) Exhaust 0·010in. (cold)
Contact breaker	0·015in. gap.
Ignition timing	10deg BTDC (stroboscopic at 650 rpm)
Spark plug	Type: Champion N9Y. Gap 0·025in.
Tyre pressures	F 22; R 24 psi (normal driving) F 26; R 28 psi (high speed) F 22; R 26 psi (full load)
Max payload	420lb (190kg)

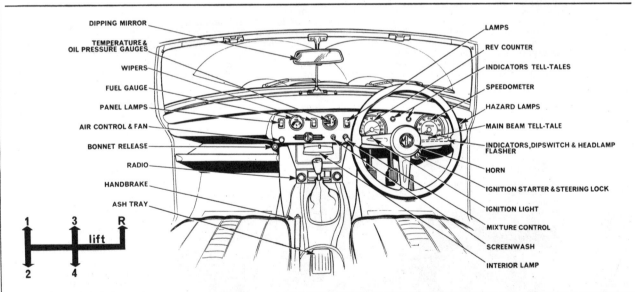

Servicing   6,000 miles

Time Allowed (hours)	3·5
Cost at £4.30 per hour	£15.05
Engine oil	£2.50
Oil Filter	£2.15
Air Filter	£1.08
Contact Breaker Points	£0.52
Sparking Plugs*	£1.48
Total Cost:	**£22.78**

*when required

Routine Replacements:	Time hours	Labour	Spares	TOTAL
Brake Pads – Front (2 wheels)	1·00	£4.30	£3.80	£8.10
Brake Shoes – Rear (2 wheels)	1·35	£5.80	£3.80	£9.60
Exhaust System	0·85	£3.65	£19.50	£23.15
Clutch (centre+driven plate)	8·00	£34.40	£12.83	£47.23
Dampers – Front (pair)	1·55	£6.65	£28.88	£35.53
Dampers – Rear (pair)	1·00	£4.30	£25.52	£29.82
Replace Half Shaft	0·55	£2.35	£13.80	£16.15
Replace Alternator	0·70	£3.00	£27.00	£30.00
Replace Starter	1·60	£6.90	£15.86	£22.76

AUTO TEST MG Midget 1500

and a live rear axle located by semi-elliptic leaf springs with no other form of assistance. It worked well enough in the past, given the Midget's very limited wheel travel, but there are signs that the latest car needs something more sophisticated to cope with its greater torque and performance.

Part of the trouble lies in the fact that the Midget, like the MGB, has been given increased ride height at the back to compensate for the greater weight of its "5 mph" bumpers and associated structure. As a result, roll stiffness at the back end has been reduced and there is much more tendency to oversteer. This is despite the heavier engine which means the front wheels bear a greater part of the total weight.

The best feature of the Midget, as always, is its very quick and accurate steering. With less than three turns of the wheel between extremes of an average 32ft turning circle, the driver never has to tie his arms in knots to turn a corner or rescue a situation. Inevitably, there is some kick-back on rough surfaces, but this is by no means the most tiring feature of the car.

Straight-line stability is no better than average, except on ultra-smooth surfaces. Normally, the Midget feels willing enough to keep to a straight course but if the wheel is released for a moment it soon reveals its willingness to wander off-line. The feeling of stability is actually due to the driver

*Massive front bumper makes the whole car look bigger than before; inset lights are well protected by lipped extensions. Door mirrors are part of standard equipment.
Headlamps are sealed-beam units, not halogen*

Standard number plate is mounted beneath the new "5 mph" bumper, rather than below the boot lid as in previous Midgets. Reversing lights are standard and boot lid can be left unlocked if the driver wishes

being barely conscious of the tiny but constant corrections he is applying.

The handling, as we have already said, holds the promise of oversteer. It is not evident at first, for in gentle driving the Midget stays very close to neutral. When driven harder into a corner, if the driver holds the wheel and accelerator steady, the tail will come out steadily until some of the lock has to be paid off before the car gets too sideways. In itself this is no bad thing, for it enables the Midget to be driven in distinctly sporting fashion by someone who knows what he is doing. At the same time it holds the seeds of danger for anyone less clever.

The real snag to the Midget's handling in 1500 form lies in its sensitivity to the throttle. Given the previous situation where the car has been wound hard into a long, tight bend, any sudden re-lease of the accelerator will bring the tail out very smartly, calling for opposite lock to pin it down. Again, this is a situation beloved of some drivers but it means the Midget is much less predictable, and certainly calls for more skill, than many small saloons of equal performance *and* cornering ability. The drawback is compounded by limited roadholding, which can leave the car well-balanced fore and aft, but skittering sideways onto a wider line than desired. Despite the increased weight and torque, the tyre section remains the same at 145–13in., and it is difficult to avoid the conclusion that the 1500 is somewhat under-tyred.

In the wet, the roadholding is considerably reduced and the Midget tends to skate around on smooth-surfaced corners. In this case, however, it is much more forgiving and the quick

steering really comes into its own.

The brakes need moderate effort and generally work well, giving a well-controlled ultimate stop of 0·95g for a pedal effort of 80lb – well within reasonable limits. The brakes have good "feel", with no sign of sponginess, and no tendency to snatch when cold. Their fade performance is less reassuring with a near-doubling of effort for a 0·5g stop during our ten-stop test, and some smell of linings towards the end; but even then there is no increase in pedal travel.

The handbrake works well, our test car recording a 0·33g stop when the handbrake was used alone on the level. It also held the car well facing either way on the 1-in-3 test hill, on which a restart was easily achieved thanks to the low first gear – but not without a smell of clutch lining.

Comfort and convenience

The Midget could hardly be described as anything but cramped, with difficult entry and exit. It has always been so, and buyers have accepted it. But the statistics tell us that Britons are getting bigger – not to say Americans – and we are surely approaching the point where it may be too small for its own good. In fact our largest staff members (the largest of all scaling 16½ stone and 6ft 2in.) found the interior space just sufficient with the driver's seat moved to its back stop, but complained of their inability to shift position to relieve numb spots. More serious were the contortions involved in getting in and out, even with the hood down.

The seats do not look especially inviting, reminding one of the shapeless BMC equipment of a few years ago. This is doing them less than justice. Together with the generally tight confines of the interior they locate driver and passenger well, and they do their best to damp out the effects of the generally mediocre ride. The ride itself will not disappoint Midget enthusiasts and could only be described, euphemistically, as "good for the liver". The limited wheel travel and high spring rates give the Midget no chance of offering a comfortable ride and the result is misery when the car is driven quickly on any uneven surface, let alone a really rough one. On the credit side it is very rare for the suspension actually to bottom, and the 1500 is notably free of the crashes and bangs which afflicted some earlier Midgets, especially when their dampers were past the first flush of youth. Nor is the handling very much affected by suspension movement, so a driver fit enough to withstand the battering can make rapid progress along almost any British road.

Bigger Triumph 1500TC engine does not look unduly large under Midget bonnet, with plenty of length to spare and room for the massive heater trunking. Access to some items is good, but others (such as battery behind heater blower unit) are difficult to reach

Above: Black crackle-finished facia panel gives slightly vintage air to the interior. Rev counter and speedometer are widely separated but can still be seen inside rim of large steering wheel. Minor dials are less easily read

Left: Midget seats look rather stylized but not very well shaped; in fact they are quite comfortable, damping out the worst effects of the ride, while the small size of the interior ensures good location. Note the awkwardly-placed door handle by the occupant's shoulder

Boot lid is supported by a single self-locking strut. Capacity is strictly limited and there is a low sill over which luggage must be lifted. Spare wheel and fuel tank lie flat on the boot floor and beneath it respectively

The controls are not well laid out, but at least they are easy to understand and are clearly labelled. There are signs of penny-pinching in the single (too slow) speed wipers, the manual-plunger washer, the primitive heater control. Of the major controls, the steering wheel is larger than one might expect and close to the chest by modern standards; the pedals are understandably close together in their narrow tunnel. Clutch effort is high but pedal movement limited, though the clutch takes up sweetly enough. In the test car, however, the accelerator linkage was rather "sudden" and no help to gentle driving. The gearchange is precise but not as quick as some of its rivals.

A major drawback of the Midget is its high interior noise level. For the most part it is made up of wind noise, which drowns the other components to the extent where one is unsure how much contribution the engine is making until one switches off and coasts at high speed. The wind noise itself comes from the hood, and while this may seem inevitable there are other soft-top cars which do not suffer in the same way (or at least, not to the same extent). In the Midget's case it is noticeable that the car is much quieter with the hood down, and the radio easier to hear, at speeds as high as 70 mph. Indeed, with the hood up the radio is almost inaudible above this speed. The

engine actually makes a lot of noise at higher speeds – it simply can't compete with the wind roar. Induction and exhaust noise is high when the car is accelerating hard, at anything over 5,000 rpm; but when the car is driven more gently the 1500 unit is quiet and refined. Noisy or not, it is very smooth right up to the red line and beyond, in a way that may surprise MG diehards.

Even with the hood up, visibility is not bad. At first sight the windscreen is shallow but it seems to provide sufficient view for short and tall drivers; the hinged quarter-lights obstruct the front-quarter view a little, but the "over-the-shoulder" blind spot is cleared by two extra windows let into the hood. Two door mirrors are standard, but on the test car they continually flopped down to a useless position. The wipers clear only a small area of screen and are too slow to cope with heavy rain. Sealed-beam headlights give good illumination at night but the driver's low eyeline prevents him making the most of it. Reversing lights are standard.

The heater is a primitive affair with a single push-pull control for temperature; and a single-speed fan which can only be switched on when full heat is selected. There is no means of selecting airflow to screen or floor, the output being shared arbitrarily. However, the fan is quiet and the heater clears the screen quickly even in humid conditions. There is no direct-flow ventilation other than via the quarter-lights.

Living with the Midget 1500

By comparison with Midget hoods of a few years ago that of the 1500 is easy to contend with. It is not yet a simple one-handed operation either to stow or erect it, though, and in particular it is much easier to fit its leading edge to the windscreen rail if four hands are available. With the hood down one does not get too battered by the airflow, even at high speed, but one driver found that when driving open in light rain the inside of the windscreen soon became covered in droplets and the occupants of the car dampened.

A basic appeal of the Midget is its simplicity, and this is still so with the 1500 which is no more difficult to work on than its predecessors. The most awkward servicing point is the need

to reach the battery at the very rear of the engine compartment under the hinge line of the bonnet; the dipstick is not easy to find, especially in the dark. A link with tradition is the need to attend to eight grease points during the 6,000-mile service – but there are no intermediate service intervals, so an average car requires only twice-a-year attention.

A main drawback of the car is its small (7-gallon) tank, which gives a safe range of less than 200 miles. It is filled via a simple cap in the rear panel, and unlike many modern tanks can be filled quickly to the brim with no danger of blow-back.

There are few accessories to be added to the Midget from the MG option list. A hardtop is expensive but might prove an investment in terms of reduced wind noise and long-journey comfort; wire wheels are available for those who can face the chore of cleaning them; and head restraints may be specified. There is no overdrive option, far less an automatic. Static seat belts are standard – apparently there is no room for inertia-reel units.

In conclusion

There is no doubt that the performance of the Midget has been greatly improved by its change of engine, and there is now a spread of torque which allows the car to be driven sportingly or to be lugged along all the way in top gear by a lazy or tired driver. At the same time the handling has suffered in some respects and the car is no longer as predictable or forgiving as it was.

People are bound to differ on how badly cramped they find the interior (though few will argue with the infuriating difficulty of reaching the interior door handles), but few would quarrel with the conclusion that the ride is harsh and the noise level over-high.

Now that the Midget and the Spitfire share the same engine, the question of their joint survival must arise. For our money – and there is scant price difference between the two – the Spitfire is much more practical and civilized. There will always be those who will scorn it for precisely those reasons, but if further rationalization comes to pass it will be difficult to make out a case for the Midget *vis-à-vis* its stablemate. □

MANUFACTURER:
British Leyland UK Ltd., Austin-Morris Division, Longbridge, Birmingham

PRICES		Insurance	Group 5
Basic	£1,333.00		
Special Car Tax	£111.08		
VAT	£115.53	**EXTRAS (inc VAT)**	
Total (in GB)	**£1,559.61**	Wire wheels	£56.12
Seat Belts, static type	(standard)	Hard top	£112.09
Licence	£40.00	Head restraints*	£18.27
Delivery charge (London)	£15.00	*Fitted to test car	
Number plates	£6.60		
Total on the Road (exc insurance)	**£1,621.21**	**TOTAL AS TESTED ON THE ROAD**	**£1,639.48**

MG Midget

Sports cars, living-legend department. Get one while they're last.

• There are lots of things you can say about an MG Midget. Like it sure is small. And it's really slow. And it's simple to the point of bare necessity. And it wanders a bit under hard braking. And it wanders a bit in crosswinds. And it is pure, unadulterated automobile fun. Most of all it's fun.

MG Midgets have been with us since late in 1928, when the M-type went into production at the old Abingdon facility. Of course there was a bit of an interruption when the Hitler war turned Britain's automobile producers to more pressing business, but within five weeks of the official end of hostilities, MG an-

nounced the first TC Midget and the string began again.

And it *was* called the TC *Midget*, and that's something to add to your collection of little-known facts that win bets in bars. But there's more. The equally famous TD and TF were also Midgets. The MGA and the MGB of more recent

vintage were of another breed altogether. And one final bit of esoterica: 10,000 MG TC Midgets were produced, and exactly 2001 exported by MG to the U.S. So the car that "started it all" in this country did so with a rather small expeditionary force.

Although that little orange Midget sitting in the *Car and Driver* parking lot right now may not seem like what a living legend should come to, it nonetheless is one. And it is also the last of its kind. In all its marketing wisdom, MG's parent company—called Jaguar Rover Triumph this week—has decided to stop Midget production this summer.

The Triumph Spitfire will be the company's only low-ball sports car.

So there you are. The end of another automotive era. Get your living legends while they're last.

Testing the Midget has turned out to be quite an adventure in automotive history. Not only is there great historical significance attached to this representative of a dying breed, the car itself is more historic than contemporary. It is the past. And if you're more of the past than of the present, any changes in the good name of technological advancement, any moves toward the contemporary will be at best only grudgingly made. Of course the Midget has a DOT-proper set of bumpers front and rear; there's a three-point harness; non-protruding rocker switches have replaced the traditional toggles; there are three wipers to ensure legal coverage of the glass; and you can bet that hidden in the doors are side-guard beams. And of course the poor thing has been forced to lug around a catalytic converter to clean its breath. But there's precious little else to indicate the Midget has been squirting off the MG production line right up to the bitter end, rather than being shoved out the door of a barn somewhere in England where the last ones were stored fifteen years ago.

To love the little dear you have to be a lover of simple machinery, because the Midget is really little more than a simple machine that happens to roll down the road on four wheels when it's doing its simple-machinery task. It is to a Chevrolet Citation what a wheelbarrow is to a Bucyrus-Erie earthmover.

To love a Midget, you have to love simple machinery. That's what it is. A simple machine that happens to be a car.

Also, to love a Midget you have to be rather supple, because slipping in through the doorway while angling your legs under the steering wheel is not a game for the creaky of joint. And the bracing, twisting, and writhing to get out are as close as you can come to automotive isometrics. It's called a Midget for a reason, you see.

Although the top goes up and down quite easily—3.5 minutes from boot-on to top-up was the time actually recorded by an agile driver caught in a sudden shower—when it's up there are spaces around the door large enough to pass a Big Mac through. And the snaps for the rear edge of the top are the same nail-breakers that broke the nails of countless TR3 owners fifteen years ago. MG's concession to modern top technology was to add a little Velcro at a couple of points where the top joins the body. Take that, revisionists.

However, top-up is the Midget at its

Continued

worst. It may be mostly psychological, but when the roof is raised, life in the Midget gets very frustrating. All the controls are too close and too close together. And it's claustrophobic in there. The windshield has about the same dimensions as a machine-gun port in a small bunker.

But put the top down and you and your Midget are transformed. Suddenly the cockpit is not only livable, it's a nice place to be. And when you move off down the road, you're not just driving, you're motoring. The little devil will cruise the world's freeways at an almost effortless 70 mph if you must. But better you should enjoy flinging it around corners in town, frightening your dog and squeezing suitable squeals out of your lady; or cruising through warm summer nights. Or maybe find a piece of countryside to charge through. And please don't worry about its taking a

With the top down, the car is transformed.

sedate sixteen seconds to get up to 60 mph, or that its quarter-mile acceleration capabilities have it in the Christmas, Slow As, category. It sounds as if it's going fast, and the tactile messages coming through the steering column are telling you you're going fast, and if your hair is whipping itself into knots and you're smiling from ear to ear, then dammit, you are going fast. Or at least fast enough. Right?

Continued

"Safety Fast" was the MG motto, but "Fun Slow" might have been more appropriate.

• The first brand-new car I ever purchased was a 1953 MG TD, metallic tan with red leather in the cockpit. I got a pair of Brooklands windscreens from Vic Derrington in England, along with a very *pur sang* Brooklands steering wheel. I sent away to Dale Runyan for a louvered hood, which I installed without the side panels and held down with a red leather strap. There was a badge bar on the front, which carried a Lucas "Flamethrower" pencil-beam road lamp and cloisonné badges for the MG Car Club, the Sports Car Club of America, the Detroit Region of the Sports Car Club of America, and the 1953 Press On Regardless Rally. A local top shop made me a zipper tonneau cover and then I painted the car white, with red underfenders, white wheels, and

a red-and-white checked grille. The *pièce de résistance* was a Boyce Motometer that actually worked, screwed into the removable radiator cap.

The engine was bored .030 oversize, the head was milled, and the ports polished. I scrounged a set of inch-and-a-half SU carburetors to replace the stock inch-and-a-quarters, and dressed them up with chromed Hellings air cleaners. The engine also wore a polished aluminum valve cover and side plate. The exhaust system was removed from the manifold back, and in its place was an inch-and-three-quarter copper straight pipe. Most of the time the pipe's song was muted by a chrome "racket buster," a short muffler that clamped onto the business end, but could be slipped off easily when my youthful blood was up.

Several of my friends owned MG TCs, and most of these were outfitted much like my TD, except that the TC had nineteen-inch wire wheels and fashion dictated that the rears be cut down to sixteen inches and, if possible, laced on a wider rim. The best TD in the world—and mine was a good one—was an innocuous little car that didn't go very fast and didn't do a very good job of keeping the rain and snow off the occupants. The TC was essentially the same, except that it didn't ride at all as a car was supposed to, and the steering required the strength of Sylvester Stallone. The TD was a better car

in almost every respect, but the TC had the advantage of the most rakish appearance seen on this side of the Atlantic since the Army Air Corps stopped flying biplanes.

We raced these cars, rallied them, ran gymkhanas and British-style trials in muddy, rocky farmland, and drove them to work every day. The fact that they were not as reliable as the American cars of the period was offset by their ease of maintenance. We did our own brake jobs, valve jobs, rebuilt the SU carburetors once a month, and got out to whack the SU fuel pump back to life every time it quit ticking, which was regularly. Our small talk dealt mainly with the vagaries of Lucas electrical systems. The fact that a T-series MG Midget was slow, heavy, and about as agile as a McCormick reaper never occurred to us. They were sports cars and we were sports. Only the arrival of significant numbers of 1500cc Porsches among U.S. enthusiast ranks caused us to doubt the ability of our little MGs to do anything we asked of them. Porsches did things that had never occurred to us. Nonetheless, the postwar Midgets rent the veil of the Detroit temple, we saw fundamental automotive truth revealed, and we never turned back. —*David E. Davis, Jr.*

MG

But alas, what it comes down to is just how much you are willing to pay for a fair-weather friend, a toy. The Midget simply isn't a serious car anymore. Sure, the heater will keep you warm, you can actually hear the radio at 70 mph, and all the bits and pieces seem to be screwed together with some thought to durability. But the Midget asks a little too much of us. The handling is really rather dodgy for today, under hard braking each wheel takes a turn at trying to get things slowed down, there's just enough room in the trunk for a cheese

sandwich, and our best guess is that after a few months of intimacy—including one old-fashioned wet, slick, and cold winter—all that nostalgia-fueled fun motoring will hardly be worth the effort. Or $5395. Pity.

There may always be an England, but this is it for Midgets. Maybe you'd better get one while they're last. And worry about winter when it gets here.

—Mike Knepper

COUNTERPOINT

• This thing is trash, and I for one won't be sad to see it go. The state of the automotive art will lurch smartly upward just from the riddance of the MG Midget. Perhaps the British will find a way to produce a few extra Spitfires or TR7s in its place, both of which I consider infinitely more desirable, price notwithstanding.

You see, the Midget never really enjoyed any development, a predicament I consider inexcusable. This car will fade from production with the same wretched, hanky-in-the-wind top it was born with. Along the way, Jaguar Rover Triumph (hey! what happened to MG?) did jack up the ride height, slap on ugly bumper masks, and drain all the horsepower out of the Midget's engine. Please excuse me if I don't consider these either improvements or developments. However, credit should be given for the compassionate excision of this car's bug-eye birth defect, and the addition of synchronizers in the transmission a few years back. In farewell, I can offer nothing more than a kick in the behind, and this goodbye to such a crude little coal cart of a car: "Get outa here, you knucklehead!"   —Don Sherman

Everything under the sun is wrong with the Midget until you put the top down; then it's perfect. With the top up, I could barely get in, much less drive, and I found that no matter how deftly I attempted to operate the various controls and switches, one or another of my knuckles and thumbs was constantly making painful contact with some other part of the little bolide. Owning a Midget is a character-building experience. One very quickly finds out whether or not one is suited for the sporting life. It is small and uncomfortable. It doesn't go very fast, nor does it handle very well. It represents about

the same level of automotive sophistication as a Japanese pickup truck. But if you're the right sort of person, none of that will make much difference when the sun is out and the top is down. And then, if you can still bear it at the end of a long, cold winter, you are destined for automotive greatness. This is where beginning car nuts get their feet wet in the sport. This is the car that introduces one to the automotive alternatives. By no stretch of the imagination is it a Porsche or a Jaguar, but it's a very nice first step in that direction, if you're tough.

—David E. Davis, Jr.

Decades ago, when God instructed the British about sports cars, He laid down an absolute formula, to be followed, no matter what, with a stiff upper lip. The design staff at MG has, by God, the stiffest upper lip this side of Alice McDaniels. But that's another story. MG's lack of progress is of no importance here, because there is no modern rationale for a little dart game like the Midget. It's not supposed to make sense and never has. This shrunken buzz bomb has got some real *whoopeee!* ballistics. It converts every tight corner, small crosswind, and big truck into a madcap change of direction, like an atomic mouse in an elephant compound. It has Woody Allen's vaguely wild-eyed approach to life, but for following Diane Keaton to the ends of the earth, you'll want something else, because this teensy car gets familiar with every corner of your body, and the seats are squishy. Forget all that. The Midget is absolutely alive and utterly tingling with the road. Every decisive move in the cockpit makes something dramatic happen. If you haven't driven an X1/9, maybe you can love a Midget. If you can fit. Maybe.   —Larry Griffin

Marathon madness

'YOU HAVE to be mad' they said . . . 'to take a Midget on the Marathon. 'You'll be out by Belgrade . . . It'll never get to Istanbul' were other firm forecasts when Roy Fidler and I announced our intention to tackle the London-to-Sydney Rally in my veteran Spridget.

Most of the entry seemed to have chosen either the comfort of a Hydrolastic 1800 or the powerful reputation of the Dagenham saloons to challenge the Australian and German contenders, so perhaps our choice was more in the way of a protest for individuality than a serious attempt to gain an outright win. However, Roy and I had a secret belief that the privateer's award *could* be won by a Midget, and for months onwards business and family life had to take a back seat while plans, designs, theories, and maps were spread thickly on every table in office and home. Work in the garage almost ceased — as far as customers were concerned anyway — and the poor storekeepers spent eight hours a day chasing after vast lists of unobtainable parts for the Midget-with-a-difference.

Without going into too many details, suspensions were hand built, bodywork was mostly replaced by identical panels in lightweight glass-fibre, and the interior was trimmed with sound resistant padding. A five-speed gearbox (which had spent two

Collector's Car, May 1980

Three wheels on my wagon... JOHN SPRINZEL on the first London to Sydney marathon. The old Midget was up to 10th place beating the works — until a wheel fell off

seasons racing in Donald Healey's Sprites) was forced into the tunnel, and Don Moore's talents were used to rebuild and balance a very standard engine. Minilite wheels — using the same tyres as the factory 1800's (for very obvious reasons) needed quite a bit of persuading to fit in the widened wheel arches, and the whole thing once assembled looked like the highest and widest Spridget in the world. Adding to this effect was the extra foot of hardtop, which incorporated three separate fuel tanks to give a total range of nearly 600 miles. Fuel stations in Turkey and Afghanistan are not exactly as plentiful as they are on the A5!

To tackle a 10,000-mile journey in so small a car did call for some sacrifices . . . carrying luggage was the first of these, and the total space allocated to personal effects allowed each person to have one toothbrush, one razor, a box of Kleenex, two spare sets of underwear, and a rally jacket. The passenger seat was replaced by a

6ft 3in bed made out of two alloy tubes, Pirelli webbing, and a Dunlopillo mattress. In addition to allowing a wide choice of reclining positions, this also enabled us to carry about 2cwt of spares *under* the bed. Apart from one throttle cable, one set of rear brake shoes, and four spark plugs, I confess that *none* of the spares were used! We even finished in Sydney with one of the tyres fitted at Crystal Palace, and only punctures forced us to change three of the others that we carried. Four gallons of water each — thickly laced with lemon and glucose, five Horlicks survival packs, and a first aid kit containing enough medicaments to doctor an army, and preparation was complete.

These few lines of typed specifications took some 1,600 hours of actual preparation — the rest of the time was spent in raising sponsors. Everyone we approached had already been tackled by Terry Hunter and Vic Elford (who had obviously been trying to earn their retirement pension out of would-be sponsors) so that our requests for £100 here and £100 there were often met with slight sighs of relief. Even so, we set off on the brightest of sunny afternoons with £800 still to find. The 'Amateurs' award was £500, and bonuses for winning it would just cover our costs.

Crystal Palace has never looked so bright, or so crowded. It seemed as if everyone had come to see the Marathon on its way, and Sir Donald Stokes stood on the start line offering all British Leyland crews £300 for finishing . . . which would really provide a slight profit if we could beat two Porsches, three Mercedes, and the horde of Cortinas and 1800's which were in private hands. Press estimates put the spactators between London and Dover at two million people — all waving like crazy — except two rather dim bluebottles organizing the biggest traffic jam I have ever seen on the exit from Vauxhall Bridge. In the end three of the foreign cars with sirens blaring made a fifth lane which took the law completely by surprise, and finally permitted 30 or so crews to at least get out of London! Terry Hunter's Porsche was stopped and a copper — in very broken German — explained that sirens were verboten. Terry in equally broken English apologized delightfully, and all was well.

Dover customs procedure was the slowest of the event — it took about 30 seconds, but then they actually *looked* at the passports. The boat trip was short and pleasant, with the calmest of seas, and our last planned sitdown meal for seven days . . . but France welcomed us with her usual official dramas. Non! we were not to use the motorway, our route should tackle a horde of the little cobbled French sideroads. Rapid consultation of the regulations confirmed that choice of route was free, so crafty back doubles and rapid approaches on side lights conned our way past the gendarmerie, and we found ourselves (in common with well over half the entry) enjoying a quiet rest down the speedy motorway to Paris. Just as well too, for the fog got thicker and thicker. By the time we reached that vast No Man's Land which counts as a frontier zone between France and Switzerland the 'pea souper' was as British as anything we had ever seen, and Roy had made his first (and only) attempt to frighten me, a Citroën driver, and the driver of a large Saviem lorry which loomed out of the fog six tenths of an inch away from my left ear. I watched with bated breath and with professional interest while Fidler added to his grey hair with a five-second display of polished cadence braking, controlled sliding, and width judging. Very interesting!

Italy demanded rally numbers to be covered — as if those gaudily painted and multi-labelled cars with dozens of lights and unwieldy 'Kangaroo guards' on the front could be *anything* other than rally cars — but the pouring rain washed away a good many of the taped up paper covers without anyone receiving penalty or penance.

Yugoslavia allowed us her motorways, the most rapid of customs ever, and a continuation of nastiness in the shape of fog, but the easy time schedules dictated by Western Europe's laws on rallying enabled the whole convoy to invade the *Hotel Metropole* at Belgrade for some 10 hours of sleep or work.

Peter Harper's fuel injected beastie had expired near Venice — with a lack of water, which seemed an odd spot for such a complaint, but this retirement also helped to prove the old rally proverb of not changing

Giant-killer arrives... 6ft 5ins of John Sprinzel clambers out of the tiny MG at Bombay — despite a top speed of 78mph, the car averaged 70mph for 23 hours to clean a timed section.

specification between test and event, for the problems were the direct cause of a repositioned pulley, altered *after* a very successful reconnaissance — and one of the top favourites was out. Schellenberg's thundering Bentley continued along the course in a blaze of publicity and noise, the occupants frozen half to death with 1930-type open-tourer ventilation. Bulgaria added no further hazards, and positioned a policeman or party official every few hundred yards — this helpful method of controlling traffic on the rally route was to be a feature of the event between Yugoslavia and India.

The Midget had given us two heartstopping moments; the first when the gearbox appeared to be using quarts and quarts of oil, (but clearing the breather pipe cured this potential disaster) and the sudden cessation of power in the midst of the *Autostrada* — near Turin at rush hour time. Fortunately this was only a broken throttle cable, and there was a spare taped neatly alongside the faulty one. Apart from these seconds of apprehension, everything was going like clockwork and no oil had been needed in the motor. Our maximum cruising speed of 78mph (which also was our maximum speed in the indirect fifth gear) gave 20mpg on the very cheapest 88 octane petrol. The mini-bed was working fabulously, and both Roy and I had had more sleep on the run through Europe than we would ever have had at home. The reclined safety harness also served to 1. hold the passenger in his chosen position, and 2. prevent the passenger from sliding that one inch to the right which would have helped to change gear.

Instanbul was unfortunately viewed at dead of night, with heavy rain streaming down, and even the trip across the Golden Horn in the Bosporus 'ferri-bot' was lacking in the expected glamour because of the moist darkness. The Turkish lorry drivers had obviously read all the terrible reports about themselves, and kept very well over to their side of the road (I think this was to the right, but customs changed so often on this trip it really was quite difficult to decide!).

The national pastime in Asia Minor is definitely tipping-lorries-up-onto-their-sides, and many picturesque views of the undersides of ancient camions are dotted along

the route. I understand that the Bentley joined in this sport, but as he was running far behind us in the convoy we were unable to inspect the nether regions of this wonderful old machine. A brave and valiant effort by a crew who were considered to be even more 'mental' than those engaged in the contest with baby sports cars.

Life for us had developed into a firm battle with Rob Slotemakers factory DAF — which improbable machine now has a Renault motor (and which was supported, it seemed, by the whole of Holland wearing green and orange uniforms while being flown around the world in the oldest Dakota still in captivity). We both seemed to have identical top speeds, except against the wind when our higher frontal aspect slowed us down to 1mph under the DAF's speed.

Roy, Rob, and I are all ex-Triumph team drivers, so that rivalry naturally continued along every inch of the route — giving the resting passenger yet another reason to bless the Britax harness!

Somewhere around here, the transcontinental-highway-tour was momentarily abandoned for a period of activity over the Sivas to Erzincan section, where Roger Clark slid into the lead hotly pursued by lots of 1800's and things. The brief 'special stage' provided a little excitement for the great control at Teheran, where the Phillips factory had laid on the most splendid facilities to revive tired crews and jaded cars.

The Ford camp were hard at it with floodlights — front suspension struts and gearboxes receiving attention, while the 1800 'pits' seemed more concerned with restocking food parcels and opting for the passenger beds rather than the driving seat. Teheran to Kabul provided a little more excitement for the works 1800's who took the shorter, rougher route and had to do a bit of repairing during the two hours they saved, and for us, who had to average just over 70mph — with a top speed of 78mph — and this for 23 non-stop hours. We buzzed in with petrol pumps ticking and two minutes only in hand after what proved to be the most tense day of the rally for us.

The barren expanse that is Afghanistan — and which really must look very much like the surface of the moon. Kabul — the capital — was the only official sleeping-halt and was the coldest spot on the route. We were surprised at the civilization which greeted us at Kabul — the hotel even had American canned beer — and we were all well fit and rested to tackle the pre-dawn classic stage over the Lataban pass. This boulder strewn pathway across the mountains is no longer in use, as a perfectly sound main road has been built along the valley, but I suppose the organizers had to sort some of us out before Bombay, if only to provide half way results for the newspapers during the long boat trip ahead.

Clark confirmed his enthusiastic skills by taking still more time from us all, but Bianchi, Lampinen, Hopkirk, and Cowan — all wearing the most civilized of touring saloons — were close behind the twin-cam racer. Australians, oddly enough, were only ahead on the bull contest — for in driving ability the best lay a distant seventh in spite of a lot of horses — but to listen to the stories (and we had about nine days of confinement ahead in which to receive the full range of tales) it was merely a matter of reaching the big dusty continent before the first six crews would disappear into the wombat holes of the Nullarbor desert.

The 1098cc Midget sets off with a lap round Crystal Palace... note the petrol tank on the roof.

The Khyber Pass was a sell-out — six bends on a good surfaced road with no steep gradients, no signs of either the ghost of Errol Flynn or of the wild tribesmen. Pakistan and India were a different story, with millions of people packing the route, defying the progress of the convoy only to part ranks at the last minute in a rather unusual game of 'chicken'.

Any halt in the progress, and the crowds descended on the cars, which though bearable in a Mercedes or 1800 was sheer hell in a Midget. The flimsy glass-fibre doors were all but torn off their hinges, both headlamp glasses broken, reverse lamps torn off the body and finally, the windscreen shattered by this unwelcomed enthusiasm. Few Marathoneers will ever forget the almost terrifying hordes through India.

After all this the boat trip on the P & O liner *Chusan* was certainly an anti-climax; more than 70 cars made it to Bombay, although only 35 had less than three hours of lateness penalty. This margin of lateness would be the maximum allowed for the first part of the Australian route, so that prophecies of only 35 at Bombay were not really so far from true. The wide margins

allowed in Europe and Asia, together with well-policed routes, speedy customs, and oft re-graded road surfaces had made the organizers planned route far easier than ever could be foretold. The Indian route from Delhi to Bombay alone had been covered with some 12 hours of time in hand, and yet the same stretch under practice conditions had penalized almost all who had surveyed what had been a road teeming with undisciplined pedestrians, trucks, and animals.

Perhaps the only thing to say of the nine day cruise was that the poker game was most interesting and, for me at any rate, quite profitable. Paddy Hopkirk summed up most of our sentiments on leaving the boat, when he told the ever-present Brian Robbins and his TV *Wheelbase* team: 'That was the best advertisement for flying I have ever seen.'

Perth welcomed us in great style. Almost the first sight as we approached was a line up of MGB's and Spridgets, with banners from the Healey and MG Car Clubs, and these same enthusiastic supporters were to drive us into the city, and later to lead us from the start to the British Leyland Service point just outside town. That our driver lost his way was perhaps unfortunate, because in almost every other way the fabulous enthusiasm and help given by this vast army of supporters was a feature of our journey through Australia. (The men of Broken Hill let the side down just a little tiny bit!).

The pattern for the final three days was soon set, with fairly easy rides through the day and early night, combined with real swinging sections around dawn, to give tired cars and tense drivers some challenging motoring. Not perhaps as tough as Liege or Safari, for the pressure just wasn't constant enough to prevent lots of repair work. The leading Cortina had so many changes of bits and pieces as it descended from the leaderboard down to 10th place, that two cannibalized versions were left by the side of the road, and few of its original vital organs remained on the car that arrived at the finish.

Marvel Lock and Lake King provided early bumps and jumps, together with more than a fair share of Australian dust. The Nullarbor was mercifully covered with fleecy clouds and had been well rained upon, leaving a cool and dust-free run over what had threatened to exhaust most of us. The Flinders ranges which followed lived up to

their threat, with plenty of close fought motoring along twisting and rough tracks much in the character of British forest roads during a dry summer.

After the Flinders we found ourselves in reach of our goal. Edgar Hermann's Porsche and the Michael Taylor Mercedes were both now behind us in the privateers battle, and with only three 'tight' sections of the rally left, it looked as if the unlikely-to-win Midget would be in the money after all.

At Broken Hill we had a small split in the front suspension mounting arc welded in expert style, and off again at high speed (78mph)! to the Menindee control. The British Leyland service team here had the most magnificent speedy jacking system, and all the 1800's were whisked four feet up into the air even before the startled crews had time to get out. Wheels were changed with lightning speed — even though hardly anybody really needed a change of tyres — but practice they had and change they would!

Our Waterloo came just 14 miles later when the front nearside wheel disappeared into the bush to join the 5,300 sheep on John Caskey's station of 45,000 acres. A quick hitch in a brave Mini Cooper back to Menindee, during which I gleaned the presence of a Midget in Broken Hill. Then a 'phone call in between the levitation acts with 1800's and the complete front unit had been stripped and brought to a waiting charter plane (not as expensive as it sounds, as everyone charters light planes out in the bush). The pilot landed on the bend of the dirt road where we were parked, but alas, the 'left side' which I had requested, had been transformed into the 'left-from-a-facing-the-front-of-the-car' and it was quite impossible to bodge up the car. Seven hours had elapsed before three brave young ladies in a Morris 1100, still happily in the rally, arrived with the correct part (it had grown too dark for the pilot to manage another trip) and with only six hours of permitted lateness, our bid for fame and fortune had gone *hors de combat*.

A night on the station, with lamb chops at every meal, and a most interesting conversation with the young couple who ran these many acres all by themselves, and then, by virtue of a little short-cutting, Sydney was reached after all. We were the only Midget with three disc wheels and one wire wheel in existence, leaving a two-wheeled Midget owner in Broken Hill quite happily clutching a set of disc pads and two IVB spotlights as a 'swop' for his entire front suspension and brake system.

That the six team 1800's all finished to take second and third place among this exotic convoy is now history, and that two very normal family saloons from Britain should take the top two places is also on the records. But that 56 crews, many of them amateurs with hardly any rally experience, should have survived such a long and often difficult journey was a tribute to the courage of the drivers and the stamina of their cars. One thing is certain, the Marathon was a success albeit a far easier one than had been planned. □

MG MIDGET

Why would anyone want one?

PHOTOS BY RON WAKEFIELD & JOE RUSZ

BACK TO BASICS is the phrase that most readily comes to mind in describing the MG Midget: It retains its unenviable position as the most basic sports car offered in the U.S. market. MG broke the barrier some 30 years ago and earned the affection of American sports-car enthusiasts, popularizing an entirely new genre of driving pleasure—small, lightweight, open 2-seater automobiles with an allure virtually unknown on this side of the Atlantic before then. There would be many other marques to follow and eventually MG's preeminent position would decline, but no other manufacturer would ever be able to take away the British carmaker's firstborn status.

The Midget was introduced in 1961 as an offshoot of the Austin-Healey Sprite Mk II, which had made its debut in Mk I ("Bugeye") form in 1958; thus the diminutive MG has one of the longest continuous production runs in the sports-car world. There have been many changes in the Midget since its birth, but it's still the same type of car it's always been: basic roadster. True, now there are windup windows, plush carpeting and other amenities scarcely dreamed of in the days of the original Midget, and U.S. safety and emission regulations have mandated many revisions and alterations, but a drive in the Midget is a nostalgic experience. Or, as the less charitable put it, the car is seriously outdated and old-fashioned.

Within the framework of the British Leyland conglomerate, the Midget shares the same inline 4-cylinder engine as the Triumph Spitfire. It's an overhead-valve design with a displacement of 1493 cc that in current form develops 50 bhp at 5000 rpm and 67 lb-ft torque at 2500 rpm. The powerplant is a workhorse "tractor-type" engine in a mild state of tune. Performance is not startling, with a 0–60 mph time of 14.3 seconds and a quarter-mile clocking of 20.3 sec at 69.5 mph (measured with our new lightweight test equipment). That 0–60 mph time is 1.2 sec

quicker than the Midget tested in June 1976, but the 1978 model is actually 0.2 sec slower in the quarter mile. Chalk that up to a reduction in compression ratio (9.0:1 down to 7.5:1) and horsepower (55.5 down to 50.0) since our 1976 test.

The Midget's 4-speed fully synchronized gearbox has a notchy feel and a high shift effort when new, but as it breaks in it improves greatly and is crisp and positive wihout being too stiff. The transmission is well matched to the engine's characteristics and makes good use of the low- and mid-range torque, enabling the Midget driver to keep pace easily with traffic around town.

A perusal of the Midget's dimensions reveals that it's aptly named, sitting on an 80.0-in. wheelbase and measuring just 143.0 in. overall. The short wheelbase, coupled with the essentially simple suspension design (lower A-arms, lever shocks as upper lateral arms, coil springs and anti-roll bar front; live axle on leaf springs with lever shocks rear), make for handling characteristics that are entertaining to some and nerve-jangling to others. One staff member described the Midget this way: "It can really be thrown about; the small size and quick reactions grow on you. The Midget's potential may be fairly low, but it's very easy to use all of that potential." Others were markedly less enthusiastic, finding the Midget something of a handful, including one person who described it in nautical terms as "very much like tacking my way up the boulevard," constantly nudging the steering back and forth to maintain a somewhat straight line. The driver who masters the Midget's handling idiosyncracies will be rewarded with some entertainment on a winding road with a smooth surface, but pushing to the limit brings about the onset of final oversteer, requiring quick driver reactions and a deft touch. The fast (2.3 turns lock-to-lock) rack-and-pinion steering also necessitates a light hand on the wheel and a bit of practice to keep from overdoing it when maneuvering.

The ride manners of the Midget are rather unpleasant. As a runabout, it's quite acceptable and the firm and jouncy nature of the car seems appropriate. For anything more than a short drive, however, the stiff-legged feel becomes tiresome.

Inside, the Midget can be described at best as cozy, at worst as claustrophobic. Perhaps it's a natural law of selection that this car is most suited to young and lithe people who don't mind contorting themselves a bit to get behind the wheel. Once there, though, they will find that leg, hip and shoulder room are restricted for anyone taller or more portly than average. The controls and instruments are well laid out and most everything (including the opposite door handle and window crank) is within easy reach—many of our staff members expressed the feeling that

it's more like wearing a car than driving one. There is insufficient space to move the seat far enough rearward for most drivers more than about 5 ft 8 in. tall; one short driver found that when the seat was close enough to depress the clutch pedal fully, she had great difficulty reaching back to use the door handle to get out! One quite serious problem concerns the safety belts—the inertia reels stick badly as you try to put on the belts, and when the convertible top is down it interferes with them so much that it becomes a major task to adjust and fit them. The reel covers won't stay on the reels, further interfering with one's good intentions to belt up. Also, the receptacles for the belt latches on the inboard side of the seats present a dangerous and hard surface to many people's hip bones. The convertible top provides

Current Midgets share their engine with the Triumph Spitfire.

MG Midget's cockpit is one of the tightest known to man.

a reasonably snug, closed environment but there is considerable wind leakage around the edges and the Midget is a car best reserved for a sunny day when the top can be left down and the driver is free to enjoy open-air motoring in the old style.

Putting the top up and down is easier than it used to be, but there are still far too many steps required, snaps to be fastened, etc. Other carmakers have found much simpler solutions to the convertible top (the Fiat 124 comes to mind) and there's no reason why British Leyland couldn't follow suit.

All in all, we find far more minuses than pluses with the MG Midget. Small, lightweight sports cars can and should be great fun to drive. Perhaps many people can and will experience that sort of fun with the Midget. But there is ever so much room for improvement, badly needed to return to MG the rightful crown as builder of exciting sports cars. As it stands, the marque has fallen into a state of disrepair.

PRICE
List price, all POE..................$4850
Price as tested $5260

GENERAL
Curb weight, lb 1835
Weight distribution (with
  driver), front/rear, % 52/48
Wheelbase, in. 80.0
Track, front/rear 46.3/44.8
Length 143.0
Width 54.0
Height 48.3
Fuel capacity, U.S. gal. 7.5

CHASSIS & BODY
Body/frame ....unit steel
Brake system ....8.3-in. discs
  front, 7.0 x 1.1-in. drums rear
Wheels .... styled steel, 13 x 4½
Tires.....................Pirelli Cinturato
  CF67, 145SR-13
Steering type .... rack & pinion
  Turns, lock-to-lock 2.3
Suspension, front/rear: lower A-arms, lever shocks as upper lateral arms, coil springs, anti-roll bar/live axle on quarter-elliptic leaf springs, lever shocks

ENGINE & DRIVETRAIN
Type ....ohv inline 4
Bore x stroke, mm........ 73.7 x 87.4
Displacement, cc/cu in. .. 1493/91.0
Compression ratio 7.5:1
Bhp @ rpm, net .... 50 @ 5000
Torque @ rpm, lb-ft .. 67 @ 2500
Fuel requirement ..unleaded, 91-oct
Transmission .... 4-sp manual
Gear ratios: 4th (1.00) 3.72:1
  3rd (1.43) 5.32:1
  2nd (2.11) 7.85:1
  1st (3.41) 12.69:1
Final drive ratio.................... 3.72:1

CALCULATED DATA
Lb/bhp (test weight) 40.1
Mph/1000 rpm (4th gear) 17.9
Engine revs/mi (60 mph) 3360
R&T steering factor 0.70
Brake swept area, sq in./ton .. 232

ROAD TEST RESULTS
ACCELERATION
Time to distance, sec:
  0–100 ft..............................3.9
  0–500 ft 10.6
  0–1320 ft (¼ mi)............20.3
Speed at end of ¼ mi, mph 69.5
Time to speed, sec:
  0–30 mph 4.4
  0–50 mph 10.2
  0–60 mph 14.3
  0–70 mph 20.7
  0–80 mph 33.4

SPEEDS IN GEARS
4th gear (4500 rpm) 85
3rd (5500) 68
2nd (5500) 47
1st (5500) 29

FUEL ECONOMY
Normal driving, mpg 28.5

BRAKES
Minimum stopping distances, ft:
  From 60 mph 189
  From 80 mph 321
Control in panic stop........very good
Pedal effort for 0.5g stop, lb 38
Fade: percent increase in pedal effort to maintain 0.5g deceleration in 6 stops from 60 mph 97
Overall brake rating..................fair

HANDLING
Speed on 100-ft radius, mph ..33.2
Lateral acceleration, g............ 0.737
Speed thru 700-ft slalom, mph....50.1

INTERIOR NOISE
All noise readings in dBA:
Constant 30 mph 72
  50 mph 81
  70 mph 86

SPEEDOMETER ERROR
30 mph indicated is actually....31.5
60 mph 60.5
70 mph 69.0

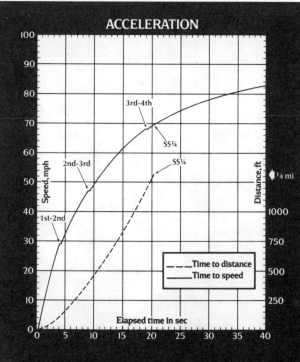

Left: The Midget — a real fun car. — in action. This is a 1974. pre-Big Bumper model; note the semi-circular rear wheel arch cut outs

Below left: Midget Mk IIIs, top in early trim and bottom after minor styling changes in 1969 Below: The final Midget variant, with US-requirement bumpers

MG Midget

FOR MORE than 50 years Britain has been the home of the small-engined sports car, and even today there is a fair choice of models on the secondhand market. In recent years, however, the business has been dominated by two cars — the MG Midget and the Triumph Spitfire — neither of which have been materially changed for some time.

In the last few months, however, the second hand business in MG Midgets has changed significantly, because the car has now gone out of production. For the first time in more than 20 years, no small-engined sports car is being built at Abingdon. A few unsold examples may still be found in new-car showrooms here, and in North America. The total stock of Midgets, therefore, must now begin to fall, and it cannot be long before

the "classic car" fever strikes.

There seems to be no chance of a "new" Midget ever being introduced, as BL spokesmen have said that they are to concentrate on the TR7 family and its derivatives in the 1980s, and that the Spitfire, too, will disappear during 1980. The Midget, they said, was dropped

because it was obsolete, because new-car sales had collapsed, and because it was far too specialised to be built profitably.

None of this, of course, affects the car's worth on the secondhand market, for nearly a quarter of a million Midgets were built from 1961 to 1979,

along with more than 129,000 of the Austin-Healey Sprites from which the Midget was derived. In terms of choice, in any case, this is a restricted sector, for the Midget's only important competitor is the Spitfire. Other cars, like the Morgan 4/4, have larger engines, and are far too costly.

Defining the pedigree

The origins of the Midget date back to 1958, and the first "frog-eye" Austin-Healey Sprite, which used modified Austin A35 engine and transmission and suspension components in a pressed-steel two-seater sports car monocoque. This car was heavily restyled in 1961 as the Mk II Sprite, and was joined by the "badge-engineered" MG Midget I. Sales and production

Left: 1975 Midget with wire wheels, an optional extra

of these mechanically identical models continued until 1971, when the Sprite was dropped.

In the meantime the engine had been increased in size twice, and in power three times. The car was given a conventional half-elliptic rear suspension, winding windows, and a great deal of detail improvement. From the end of the 1960s, however, the only other major change has been an engine transplant and controversial restyle in 1974. Purely to keep this survey within bounds, therefore, we are going to limit coverage to the Mk III models of 1966-1974, and the 1500s built from 1974 until fairly recently.

All Midgets (and Austin-Healey/Austin Sprites built until 1971) had a small and distinctly narrow two-seater open sports car body layout, with independent front suspension and a live axle suspended on half-elliptic leaf springs. All had rack-and-pinion steering and front wheel disc brakes. Usually they were sold with "build-up" sports car hoods, but detachable hardtops were also available, either from

Much of the boot space was occupied with the spare wheel, jack and tonneau cover

the factory, or from specialist concerns.

All cars had four-cylinder overhead valve engines; Mk IIIs used BMC A-Series units of 1,275c.c., and 1500s used Triumph engines of 1,493c.c. in each case matched to appropriate gearboxes.

Engines and transmissions

From 1966 to 1979 there were only two types of engine and transmission fitted to Midgets. All Mk III models (and all equivalent Sprites) were powered by the BMC A-Series 1,275c.c. engine, which delivered 65 bhp (net) at 5,800 rpm. This was the final derivative of a design first sold in 1951 (when it was an 803c.c. unit), and is still in large-scale production in different forms for cars like the Mini, the Allegro and the Marina ranges. It is worth recalling that the very first Sprites had 948c.c. and 43 bhp. The 1,275c.c. engine was

matched to a BMC four-speed gearbox which had an equally long history, and which had an un-synchronised first gear; with this gearbox, the reverse was to the right and alongside the top gear position.

Because the Midget largely existed by courtesy of demand from North America, it had to be modified to keep abreast of the changes in exhaust emission requirements in that continent. The BMC engine could not be up-dated to meet the 1975-model laws, so it was replaced by the Triumph Spitfire 1,493c.c. engine which produced 66 bhp (DIN) at 5,500 rpm. This engine was almost as venerable, as it dated from 1953 (and 803c.c.), and is still being built for the existing Triumph Spitfire, and (in a different form) for the Dolomite 1300 and Dolomite 1500 saloons. The Triumph engine was matched to the all-synchromesh Spitfire gearbox (with reverse to the right and alongside the third gear position) and had rather wider-spaced intermediate ratios.

Axle ratios remained unchanged throughout, and (unlike the rival Spitfire) there was no overdrive option. Similarly, and obviously with such a small car, there was no automatic transmission option.

Body choice and equipment changes

Basically there are no significant differences between a 1966 Mk III Midget and the last of the 1500s built in 1979. No important restyling was carried out, in fact, between 1961 and the end of the 1970s, which means that all the cars under consideration had the same small two-seater body, with a cramped cockpit offering only 48 inches of across-shoulder space.

From time to time, however, there were detail changes. In the autumn of 1969, style changes included standardization of Rostyle road wheels, the use of safety-type rocker switches on the facia, and the inclusion of reclining seats, and carpeted floors. In January 1972, too, the fuel tank was increased in size, from six gallons to seven gallons (but the overall range was still very restricted), while a locking glove box was standardized, and the rear wheel arch cut out became semi-circular in section.

The most sweeping change came in the autumn of 1974, when the Triumph 1,493c.c. engine was standardised. To meet North American safety legislation, large black polyurethane bumpers took the place of the conventional chrome items, and at the same time the rear wheelarch cutouts reverted to their flattened style

of 1961-1971! Of more importance (because it reduced the car's roadholding) was the fact that the overall ride height was increased by a full inch, again for safety regulations reasons.

Performance and Economy

It was predictable that when the Triumph engine was slotted into the Midget, there was an outcry from enraged MG "purists". They were quite wrong. In spite of the Midget 1500's increased weight, it is significantly quicker than any Mk III Midget, and really no less economical. Secondhand buyers, therefore, are on the horns of a dilemma. If they want what some people consider to be "pure" Midgets, they will have to buy a Mk III, but if they don't mind the looks of the 1500, or the less-responsive roadholding, they should certainly buy a Midget 1500.

The ideal, of course, would be a 1500-engined Mk III, but such cars do not exist, and it would be difficult if not

impossible to rebuild a Mk III into that condition.

It should be remembered, of course, that all these remarks apply to cars built for the British market. In North America, for instance, there is absolutely no doubt that the Midget 1500 is much quicker than the MK III, as the 1,275c.c. engine, in its final years, suffered badly from strangulation by North American exhaust emission regulations.

It is worth remembering that many Midgets will have been further tuned by their first owners, so you could possibly find a Mk III which is rather

BODY AND ENGINE AVAILABILITY

Model	Mk III	1500
1,275 c.c. (65 bhp at 5,800 rpm)	1967-74	—
1,493 c.c. (66 bhp at 5,500 rpm)	—	1975-1980

APPROXIMATE SELLING PRICES

	MkIII 1,275c.c.	1500 1,493c.c.
£550—£600	1970	
£700—£750	1971	
£850—£900	1972	
£1,000—£1,050	1973	
£1,200—£1,300	1974	
£1,400—£1,500		1975
£1,700—£1,800		1976
£2,000—£2,100		1977
£2,400—£2,500		1978
£2,800—£2,900		1979

Note: *There were no engine or transmission options of any nature, except that the engine type was changed in autumn 1974*

CHASSIS IDENTIFICATION

		Series	Chassis No.
October 1966: Midget Mk III with 1,275 c.c. engine announced. (Austin-Healey Sprite Mk IV was mechanically identical) First chassis numbers:	Midget III	G/AN4	52412
	Sprite IV	H/AN9	64756
October 1969: Minor style changes, including use of Rostyle wheels. First chassis numbers:	Midget III	G/AN5	74886
	Sprite IV	H/AN10	85287
January 1971: Austin-Healey now to be known as Austin, from:	Sprite IV	H/AN10	86802
July 1971: Sprite derivative finally discontinued at	Sprite IV	H/AN10	87824
January 1972: Changes for 1972, including round-section rear wheel arches, and larger fuel tank.	Midget III	G/AN5	105501
September/October 1974: Mk III discontinued, in favour of Midget 1500, with Triumph 1,493c.c. engine, and big black "soft" bumpers. Final chassis:	Midget III	G/AN5	153920
First 1500 chassis:	Midget 1500	G/AN6	154101
Summer 1979: Midget discontinued (but cars in showrooms until spring 1980). Final chassis number:	Midget 1500	G/AN6	

Note: *The change over came in October 1974, and was accompanied by styling changes. All MK IIIs had chrome bumpers while all 1500s with 1,493c.c. engines had black plastic deformable bumpers.*

faster than our test figures suggest. On the other hand, such a car may be significantly less economical, and less flexible in heavy traffic.

Model availability and choice

Between 1966 and 1974, 86,650 Mk IIIs were built, and these were followed by about 72,000 Midget 1500s; in addition, of course, there were more than 24,000 cars badged as Austin-Healeys (1966-1970) or merely as Austins (1971 only). Even allowing for the fact that the vast majority, over 80 per cent, of all these cars were exported — mainly to North America — there should be a good selection of cars on the secondhand market. Apart from differences in colour and trim, the only real choice of specification may be whether or not the optional hardtop, or the optional wire spoke wheels are specified. It may also be worth noting that inertia-reel safety belts were not standardized before 1977, and that dual-circuit braking was not standardized until 1978.

Not only should you look for these cars at British Leyland dealerships, particularly those which have been connected tith the MG franchise for some years, but at one of the numerous sports car specialist dealers throughout the country. There is also a healthy private trade in these models, especially in the motor sporting periodicals.

At the moment, prices and values are fairly predictable, though in future it is likely that some first owners will try to trade on the ''classic'' and ''scarcity value'' aspect. But until supplies really begin to diminish later in the 1980s, this attitude will not be justified.

Spares and Service

Getting service for a Midget should present no problems, as long as you patronize one of the BL specialist dealers, and as the car has only just gone out of production (and the main engine/transmission units are still being made for the Spitfire) there should be absolutely no problem over the supply of spares. In terms of body and trim items, however, there are enough minor sub-divisions to make an accurate quotation of your vehicle chassis number imperative at all times.

SPECIFICATION AND PERFORMANCE

	Mk III	Mk III	1500
Tested in *Autocar* of:	9 Feb 1967	4 Feb 1971	14 June 1975
Specifications:			
Engine size (c.c.)	1,275	1,275	1,493
Engine power (DIN bhp)	65	65	66
Car length	11ft. 5.4in;	11ft. 9in.	for 1500
width		4ft. 6.9in.	
height		4ft. 0.6in	
Boot capacity (cu. ft.)		7.0	
Turning circle (kerbs)		31ft. 6in.	
Unladen weight (lb)	1,589	1,546	1,720
Max. payload (lb)	350	350	420
Performance:			
Mean maximum speed (mph)	94	94	101
Acceleration (sec):			
0-30mph	4.6	4.2	3.7
0-40mph	7.0	6.5	5.8
0-50mph	9.9	9.6	8.5
0-60mph	14.6	14.1	12.3
0-70mph	20.7	20.0	17.0
0-80mph	33.2	29.7	24.0
0-90mph	—	51.3	35.3
Standing ¼-mile (sec)	19.7	19.6	18.5
Consumption:			
Overall mpg	28.4	29.6	27.9
Typical mpg—easy driving	37	38	36
Typical mpg—average	31	33	31
Typical mpg—hard driving	26	27	25
mpg at steady 70 mph	31.7	35.7	29.8
Fuel grade	4-star	4-star	4-star
Oil consumption (mpp)	800	1,200	1,000

Above: The small two-seater body had a rather cramped cockpit offering only 48in of across shoulder space
Below: Interior facia remained much the same although in later models the toggle switches were changed to rocker type

SPARES PRICES

	Mk III 1,275 c.c.	1500 1,493 c.c.
Engine assembly-bare (new)	£510.60	£359.95
Gearbox assembly (new)	n.a.	£272.55
Clutch pressure plate	n.a.	n.a.
Clutch driven plate (new)	£11.47	£15.99
Propellor shaft universal joint repair kit (each)	£5.06	£5.06
Final-drive assembly (new)	£93.15	£286.35
Brake pads — front (set, new)	£9.65	£9.65
Brake shoes — rear (set, new)	£8.72	£8.26
Suspension dampers — front (pr)	£36.93	£36.93
Suspension dampers — rear (pr)	£22.94	£22.94
Radiator assembly (new)	£69.18	£69.18
Alternator (new)	£41.77	£41.77
Starter Motor (exc)	£22.38	£22.38
Front wing panel	£64.40	£49.45
Bumper, front (new)	£6.95	£64.40
Bumper, rear (new)	£47.73	£76.48
Windscreen, toughened	£17.83	£17.83
Windscreen, laminated	£27.71	£27.71
Exhaust system complete	£43.12	£55.89

All the above prices include VAT at 15 per cent.

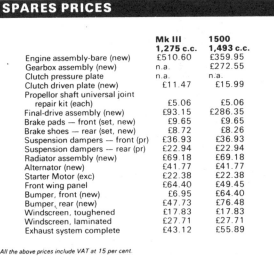

There were only two types of engines available; the 1,275 c.c. MBC A-Series (right); and the 1,493 c.c. Triumph Spitfire engine (far right)

What to Look For

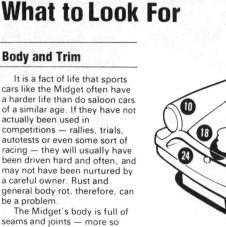

Body and Trim

It is a fact of life that sports cars like the Midget often have a harder life than do saloon cars of a similar age. If they have not actually been used in competitions — rallies, trials, autotests or even some sort of racing — they will usually have been driven hard and often, and may not have been nurtured by a careful owner. Rust and general body rot, therefore, can be a problem.

The Midget's body is full of seams and joints — more so than usual for its original design was done on a "minimum-tooling" basis. Externally, however, look for rust on the sill under the doors (1), especially at the joint with the floor (2), and at the front (3) and rear (4) of these panels. Look for rust at the door hinge pillars (5), and at the base of the pillar/sill joint (6). Hidden away, but still critical, are the rear suspension spring supports (7) which are especially vulnerable, the inner rear wheel arches (8), and the seams involved in front wheel arch foldings (9). There is also a fair chance of rust around the headlamp holes (10), around the edges of the wheel arches (11), and at the base of the scuttle panel where it joins the floor pan. In all these cases, severe structural rot means that you should not even consider buying the car, though external deterioration can be dealt with (at a price).

Hoods often bear the marks of neglect (12) and frequent furling and unfurling; at least, in this case, replacement is easy, and not too expensive. Cars like

this often have neglected coachwork, especially in the boot area (13), so look inside the boot for evidence of neglect, of damage due to loose objects, or perhaps due to water leaks and even oil spillage. Damage to carpets or seats (14) is a particular worry with this car, because the quality was none-too-high, and because it was such a difficult car to get into and out of that scuffing was almost inevitable.

Mechanical

Although the engines themselves are robust, and have a good reputation, the suspensions come in for criticism. Start by checking the condition of front (15) and rear (16) dampers, which seem to wear out, or become soft, quite rapidly, then go on to consider bush and trunnion wear (17) in the A35-based front suspension. That, and ball-joint wear of the steering linkage (18) is often present, may affect the handling, and of course may

lead to heavy tyre wear.

At the same time, check underneath the car for possible repair after accident damage (19), because this car's chassis is always likely to have been distorted in a nose-end shunt. The brakes on Midgets are small relative to the performance of the car, and may wear quickly if the car is habitually driven hard; check for front disc wear or scoring (20). In all such cases, a test drive should include a check for straightline running, especially when driven "hands-off" on an uncambered road.

There is little to be said about the BMC 1,275c.c. engine, except to point out that in spite of its power output it is still a de-tuned derivative of the Cooper S unit from which it evolved and so is a solid little unit. Even the more highly-tuned models if properly serviced and maintained, seem to have long lives, and it is only the usual signs of high oil consumption and even more

valve noise than normal which will give a clue to a worn out engine.

The Triumph engine, too, may go for up to 100,000 miles without a mishap, but with this engine, as with the 1,275c.c. unit, look carefully for the condition of the clutch (21), which may already have had a hard life.

In each case, gearboxes start life when new as rather noisy installations, and become more so with age. Look for noisy lower gears (22), and worn out second gear synchromesh (23) There should be no excessive free play in the differential mechanism even though they are normally by no means silent in operation.

A general inspection for all signs of previous use in some form of competition (24) may be instructive. Look for things like fixing holes for extra lamps, extra instruments, roll cages, and the tell-tale re-painting caused after decals or other stick on patches have been removed. No matter how good the general design of car, no Midget is any the more desirable for having been used to its limits by a previous owner.

BROOKLANDS BOOKS

MGA & MGB

MG MGB 1962-1970

A total of 10 road tests, plus comparison tests, a 45,000 mile report and used car tests together with articles on new model introductions, tuning, Le Mans, the Taurus and Janspeed MGB, and manufacturing. All model MGB roadsters up to 1970 are covered including the 3 & 5 bearing engines and the automatic.
100 Large Pages.

MG MGB 1970-1980

Over thirty articles covering the following topics. Road tests, comparison tests, used car tests, new model introductions, design proposals, history, choosing a used MGB, rebuilding, supertuning, race preparation, service testing, investment and driving impressions, models covered include the MK I & MK II & MK III. Roadsters with manual & automatic drive.
100 Large Pages.

MG CARS 1959-1962

This book deals with all MG models in production between 1959 and 1962, and there are comprehensive road tests on the MGB from Autocar and Car & Driver and introductory articles from Autosport and Motor. Other models covered in this book include the MGA, Midget, Magnette 1100 & articles cover road tests, road research reports, racing, used car tests and history.
100 Large Pages.

MGB GT 1965-1980

A total of 8 road tests and 31 articles covering the GT version of this popular classic car. Topics covered are, buying secondhand, used car tests, comparison tests, driving impressions, 12,000 and 24,000 mile reports, new model introductions, factory visits and drivers reports. All MGB GT models are reported on including the Berlinette, the Castello and the V8.
101 Large Pages.

MG MGA 1955-1962

The most comprehensive Brooklands title on the MGA. Some 8 road tests are included in the 35 articles. Other stories cover driving reports, new model introductions, a used car test, record breaking, Le Mans, a 30,000m report and a comparison test between the TR3A and Twin-Cam. Models covered are the roadster, coupé, EX 179, 181 and 182, plus the 1600, MkII, and Twin-Cam.
100 Large Pages.

MGA Collection No. 1 (1955-1982)

A total of 24 articles drawn from the US, Britain and Australia. Besides 6 road tests there are articles on touring, history, record breaking and new model reports, plus advice on buying a used model, rebuilding and tuning. Models covered are the roadster, coupé, 1600, MkII, Twin-Cam and EX 181.
70 Large Pages.

These soft-bound volumes in the 'Brooklands Books' series consist of reprints of original road test reports and other stories that appeared in leading motoring journals during the periods concerned. Fully illustrated with photographs and cut-away drawings, the articles contain road impressions, performance figures, specifications, etc. <u>NONE OF THE ARTICLES APPEARS IN MORE THAN ONE BOOK.</u> Sources include Autocar, Autosport, Car, Cars & Car Conversions, Car & Driver, Car Craft, Classic & Sportscar, Modern Motor, Motor, Motor Manual, Motor Racing, Motor Sport, Practical Classics, Road Test, Road & Track, Sports Car Graphic, Sports Car World and Wheels.

From specialist booksellers or, in case of difficulty, direct from the distributors:
BROOKLANDS BOOK DISTRIBUTION, 'HOLMERISE', SEVEN HILLS ROAD,
COBHAM, SURREY KT11 1ES, ENGLAND. Telephone: Cobham (09326) 5051
MOTORBOOKS INTERNATIONAL, OSCEOLA, WISCONSIN 54020, USA.
Telephone: 715 294 3345 & 800 826 6600

SPRIDGEBITS LTD.
THE SPRITE-MIDGET SPECIALISTS

We are leading specialists in the supply of spare parts for all Sprites and Midgets built from 1958 to 1979. On the merchanical side, we can offer everything that wears out in the front suspension, such as wishbones, kingpins, discs and shock absorbers. Inboard of these, we stock steering racks and radiators; moving aft reconditioned engines and gearboxes. For the rear end, we can offer a similarly comprehensive range of parts.

To hold these bits together, we carry a wide range of body parts; complete panels — even for the Frogeye — and an ever-increasing range of purpose-made sections. To beautify your interior, we offer an unparallelled range of internal trim from recovered seats and carpets right down to door check straps. To keep the weather out, we can provide you with hoods, tonneaus and hardtops. For the outside, you can choose from a range of reconditioned wheels and find those last details such as badges, mirrors and wiper blades.

If you're still not convinced of the breadth of our range — well, we also carry a full range of service parts from clutches to cylinder repair kits, accessories such as boot-racks and locking wheel nuts, in addition to a range of tuning parts. Finally, as we also have the largest stock in the U.K. of secondhand Spridget spares don't forget that this always provides a cheaper — and sometimes the only-way of getting the part you want.

We buy and sell cars, both sick and healthy and we're always ready to offer you technical (and non-technical!) advice — there isn't a great deal we don't know about Sprites and Midgets!

We operate a full mail order service, including export and accept credit card orders. Our comprehensive catalogue is available free on request; as it's constantly being up-dated, send for a current copy. We have now moved! For all enquiries contact:

SPRIDGEBITS LTD.
The Birmingham MG Centre,
121/123 Church Hill Road,
Handsworth, Birmingham B20
Tel: 021-554 2033

SPRITE & MIDGET

AUSTIN HEALEY SPRITE 1958-1971

Some 32 articles lead us through Sprite development from the introduction of the 'bug-eye' in 1958. Stories are drawn from Canada, the US, Australia and Britain. There are 11 road tests a 'spot check', a road research report, a comparison with the Honda S800 and a Road & Track Used Car Classic rundown. Models covered include the MkI, MkII, MkIII, MkIV, the Sebring and cars prepared by Warwick, Gaston and Alexander.

100 Large Pages.

AUSTIN HEALEY 'FROGEYE' SPRITE Collection No. 1. (1958-1961)

A total of 23 stories drawn from the US, Australia and the UK make up this book. They include 5 road tests, 2 used car reports, 3 articles on rebuilding, history, and cover a supercharged model plus the one Sammy Davis drove for over 120,000 miles.

70 Large Pages.

MG MIDGET 1961-1980

Fifteen road tests are included in the 33 stories that lead us through the development of the last of the MG Midgets. Other pieces include a comparison test vs. a Spitfire, articles on rallying, history, new model reports, tuning and an excellent guide to buying a secondhand car. Models covered include the Mk.I, Mk.II, Mk.III and the 1500.

100 Large Pages.

These soft-bound volumes in the 'Brooklands Books' series consist of reprints of original road test reports and other stories that appeared in leading motoring journals during the periods concerned. Fully illustrated with photographs and cut-away drawings, the articles contain road impressions, performance figures, specifications, etc. NONE OF THE ARTICLES APPEARS IN MORE THAN ONE BOOK. Sources include Autocar, Autosport, Car, Cars & Car Conversions, Car & Driver, Car Craft, Classic & Sportscar, Modern Motor, Motor, Motor Manual, Motor Racing, Motor Sport, Practical Classics, Road Test, Road & Track, Sports Car Graphic, Sports Car World and Wheels.

From specialist booksellers or, in case of difficulty, direct from the distributors:
BROOKLANDS BOOK DISTRIBUTION, 'HOLMERISE', SEVEN HILLS ROAD, COBHAM, SURREY KT11 1ES, ENGLAND. Telephone: Cobham (09326) 5051 MOTORBOOKS INTERNATIONAL, OSCEOLA, WISCONSIN 54020, USA. Telephone: 715 294 3345 & 800 826 6600